**Biddy Baxter, Edward Barnes
and John Adcock devised and wrote the
BLUE PETER BOOK**

CONTENTS

4 Hello There
6 Hello Sailor!
9 Lord Nelson's Funeral
11 Brazil
15 Face to Face
18 Souper Spud!
21 Potage à la Parmentier
22 Fit for a Queen
25 Handy Holders
26 How I Joined Blue Peter
28 Do you have a problem?
29 Paddington Passes Through
34 Key-Note Appeal
37 Mystery Picture
38 Long time No Sea
41 Simon and Goldie
43 The man who invented Akela
46 Christmas Glitter
48 "Unst upon a time...."
51 The Case of the Cup that Cheers
54 The Secret Life of Lucy Mathen
58 Goodbye Petra
62 V.I.P.S.
63 Seeing Stars
65 Pete Goes to Knight School
68 Knights of Blue Peter
70 Ski Marathon
73 Trapeze
76 Solutions & Useful Information
77 Competition & Blue Peter Party

£1.35

Hello There!

Here's our 15th Blue Peter Book and it's full of news of what we've been doing for the past year.

It's probably been our busiest ever, with Pete filming for his new *Blue Peter Special Assignment* series which you'll be able to see in the autumn, and working on *Stop Watch* and *We're Going Places,* and John and Shep preparing for six new *Go With Noakes,* and John's return to the theatre after 12½ years.

But the biggest news of all is welcoming Simon and our new puppy, Goldie. We had hundreds of letters from people all over the country wanting to join Blue Peter, and quite a lot of them asked what qualifications were needed. Well, how *do* you get on to a television programme? If you turn to page 26, you can find out how Simon joined. And look out for the photos of Blue Peter's very first Golden Retriever on pages 41 and 42.

It was a momentous occasion when we helped to put up William Timym's beautiful bronze statue of Petra in its place of honour by our front gates at Television Centre. It's thanks to you that it happened, because after Petra died, literally thousands of people suggested that a statue would be a good way of remembering Britain's most famous dog.

Two more awards have joined our collection. Viewers of *Multicoloured Swap Shop* voted for Blue Peter as their favourite programme, and for John as their favourite Children's Television Personality. And *Go With Noakes* and the Christmas *All Star Record Breakers* in which we all took part, won the British Academy of Film and Television Arts Star Awards. But these all take a very second place to the Silver Medal for Gallantry and the Vellum Certificates awarded to the helmsman and crew of Blue Peter IV, our Inshore Lifeboat station at St Agnes in Cornwall. David Bliss, Barry Garland and Roger Radcliffe rescued an injured surfer in what the official citation described as 'impossible' conditions. And David's Silver Medal is only the seventh ever to be awarded to any Inshore Lifeboat man.

So much has been going on, we couldn't pack it all into this book, but what with our Trapeze lesson, Jousting, the Ski Marathon, and Cleaning Admiral Lord Nelson we hope it's a record of some of *your* favourite Blue Peter happenings.

And if you've any ideas about what you'd like to see in our sixteenth book, drop us a line and we'll do our best to include them.

John Noakes   Lesley Judd.

Shep   Jack   Jill

Peter Purves   Simon Groom   Goldie

4

DO YOU RECOGNISE ANY OF THESE PHOTOGRAPHS?

THEY'VE ALL BEEN IN BLUE PETER. TURN TO PAGE 76 FOR THE ANSWERS.

HELLO SAILOR!

I was making the RAF gymnast film when I got the message. After a day and a half with the best gym display team in Britain, my back was breaking and my knees were turning to jelly when someone said:

"There's a phone call for you from London!"

"Who is it?" I asked.

"The man upstairs," they replied.

They meant my boss back at the Television Centre. He doesn't phone me much, but when he does, it usually means trouble.

"Johnny," he said. "I was driving home through Trafalgar Square last night and I saw a ladder running up to the top of Nelson's column."

"Why didn't you climb up it and jump off?" I thought, but what I said was: "Oh, really?"

"I wondered if you'd fancy climbing up like you did in 1968?" said the man upstairs.

"Hang on a minute—there was scaffolding all round the column then. It wasn't just a single ladder!"

"Quite right," he said. "This one will be a much better story. The crew will meet you at 8 o'clock tomorrow morning at the foot of the column. Goodbye!"

I discovered that they were cleaning up Nelson because he stands right on the Jubilee route. In a few days' time, the Queen would be driving through Admiralty Arch in the golden Coronation Coach, and no one wanted Her Majesty to look up between waves and see Britain's greatest sailor covered in pigeon droppings. Reg Dosell, one of London's top steeplejacks, was put in charge of the operation and he was the first person I spoke to when I arrived in Trafalgar Square on a thundery May morning.

"I don't reckon much of the weather," I said hopefully, looking up at Lord Nelson, silhouetted against a black sky. "Do you think we should call it off?"

"No, it's all right," grinned Reg. "He's got his own lightning conductor. I know because we've tied our ladders on to it!"

"Thank you for nothing," I thought, noting the series of flimsy-looking ladders lashed on to an even flimsier looking lightning-conductor which ran to the top of the column.

This was the easy bit! I reached the first plinth to join cameraman Terry Doe and Steeplejack Reg Dosell.

The next stage was a bit trickier.... The short ladder onto the plinth leant backwards about 20 degrees and the overhang was 27 metres from the Trafalgar Square traffic.

"The most important thing," said Reg, as he helped me with my climbing belt, "is to stop before you get too tired. When you get tired you lose control of your muscles and that's when it gets dangerous. If you have to stop, clip yourself on with this." He indicated a giant-sized dog clip on the front of the belt. "O.K., John? I'll lead the way."

Reg was one of those lovely, big, calm, capable men, that I knew I could trust from the moment I set eyes on him. It's having confidence in men like Reg Dosell that has given me the nerve to attempt some of the daft things I've done while I've been on Blue Peter.

The first part of the climb took us up on to the base platform just above the lions where politicians sometimes make speeches when there's been a rally. I wasn't too worried about that bit because I've seen people like Michael Foot and the Prime Minister up there—and they're even older than me!

But once I was on the platform, there was nothing but 16 metres of column between me and Nelson. Cameraman Peter Chapman was at the bottom filming the start, and Terry Doe was already at the top getting bird's-eye-view shots of me as I climbed.

When I was halfway up, I remembered the punishment I'd taken with the Gym Display team the previous day. My knees started knocking, and my arms felt as though they would be wrenched out of their sockets at any moment.

I looked up and saw Reg almost at the top, and remembering his warning, I clipped my dog clip on to the ladder and waited for my arms and legs to stop shaking.

The second half was not so bad, but when I got underneath Nelson, I saw the extent of the overhang. The short ladder onto the plinth not only leant backwards about 20 degrees, but slewed 15 degrees to one side to get round the coping at the top of the column. That really did give me the nasty sickly feeling in my groin, and I kept thinking that in a few minutes' time I'd be doing it again—only backwards!

"This is the awkward part," said Reg, as though he was talking about a stepping-stone over a stream.

I remembered how magnificent the view was from the last time. You could see Big Ben framed right between Nelson's legs, St James's Park, and Buckingham Palace, looking like a doll's house, lay over to the right; and on the left, as the river snakes down to the city, St Paul's, where Nelson is buried.

I hadn't met Terry Doe before. He was a young assistant cameraman, bursting with enthusiasm.

"When you go over in the Bosun's chair, John, I can drop alongside and get the most terrific shot . . ."

But I'd had enough. My back was killing me, and I wanted to save all my energy for the climb down. I told him, and his face fell a mile.

"All right, Johnny—I'll start packing up my gear."

I couldn't stand it. His look of disappointment was harder to bear than the chance of falling into the fountain.

"All right then, Reg," I said, "let's get the Bosun's

chair on."

The Bosun's chair is a rope cradle which allows the climber to lower himself a few inches at a time by manipulating the two knots. It's perfectly safe, provided you keep your head and don't panic.

"Just get comfortable," said Reg. "Before you go anywhere, get comfortable."

Reg dropped me slowly over the edge.

. . . Never mind, no one will notice.

By gum, his hat's a bit dirty . . .

I knelt in an attitude of prayer on the side of the plinth and gradually allowed myself to sink back into the cradle, and slowly over the side of the platform until I was dangling, like a puppet on a string, 27 metres above London. Terry came down on one side of me and Reg on the other.

"Move your knot six inches down the rope—and push your body down—that's the way."

The rope gave a sickening lurch—I looked down at the tiny figures in the square and thought that there must be easier places to learn the techniques of the Bosun's chair.

I helped Reg to knock some of six hundredweight of pigeon droppings that had accumulated in the nine years since I was there before, and inched my way slowly back onto the plinth.

The plinth, however, is not the top. There was one more ladder which ran up the back of Nelson himself to his hat at the summit. I suppose it's daft, but I couldn't resist going up that bit farther until I could put both hands on the corners of his Admiral's hat.

"I'll never do that again," I thought, as I peered over the top and watched the Dinky toy buses disappearing down Whitehall, "but mind you, I said that last time!"

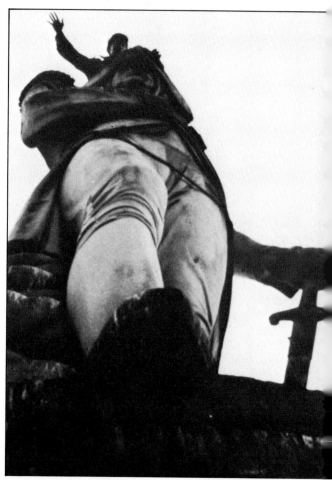

LORD NELSON'S FUNERAL

When I went to Portsmouth, I stood on HMS *Victory*, Nelson's flagship at the glorious Battle of Trafalgar. I wondered what happened after the battle, and I uncovered a strange story.

Lord Nelson, Commander in Chief of the British fleet, was the hero of all the British people and of the Royal Navy. All the seamen were horrified to see him shot down on the deck of his flagship by a French sniper.

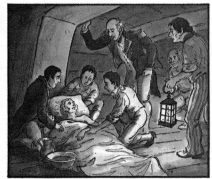

21 OCTOBER 1805. TRAFALGAR DAY
Nelson heard the news of his victory as he lay dying. "Don't throw me overboard," he murmured. The officers knew the nation would want to honour Nelson with a great state funeral.

21 OCTOBER—9.00 PM
His body was put in a cask containing brandy, to preserve it on the voyage home. The seamen insisted that Nelson must travel on his own flagship—but *Victory* was badly damaged.

28 OCTOBER—TRAFALGAR PLUS 7
So she put in to Gibraltar, where the most urgent repairs were carried out, while the Admiral lay ashore, guarded night and day.

4 NOVEMBER—TRAFALGAR PLUS 14
She put to sea again, with Nelson aboard and his colours at half-mast. It was wild, blustery weather, and many seamen must have wondered if they would drown.

3 DECEMBER—TRAFALGAR PLUS 43
After a perilous voyage, *Victory* reached Portsmouth, her home port. She was towed through the Channel fleet, as seamen stood on her decks, cheering *Victory*, yet weeping for the death of Nelson. *Victory* lay off Portsmouth whilst plans were made for the most splendid funeral London had ever seen.

10 DECEMBER—TRAFALGAR PLUS 50
At last she set sail on her last journey with Nelson on board, along the coast of Britain, towards the Thames estuary.

21 DECEMBER—TRAFALGAR PLUS 61
She was greeted by the Admiralty yacht *Chatham*, with the Lords of the Admiralty on board. Nelson's body was transferred to a coffin made from the wood of a French ship he had captured years before. Nelson's flag was struck from the *Victory* and transferred to the *Chatham*, to fly at half-mast as she sailed to Greenwich.

1 JANUARY 1806—TRAFALGAR PLUS 72
There the body lay in state in the great Painted Chamber of the Royal Naval Hospital, surrounded by flags and battle honours.

8 JANUARY—TRAFALGAR PLUS 79
Nelson's last voyage was made in the gilded state barge of King Charles II, at the head of a waterborne procession to Westminster. Then the coffin was taken to the Admiralty in Whitehall, where it rested overnight.

THURSDAY, 9 JANUARY 1806—TRAFALGAR PLUS 80
The funeral took place. Nelson's body was drawn through the streets of London on an enormous funeral car, escorted by 300 men from the *Victory*, men from every regiment stationed near London, 160 carriages and all the princes of the Royal family, to be buried with great honour under the dome of St Paul's Cathedral. Home was the sailor, home from the sea—at last!

Our first ever expedition to the South American continent began in one of the world's most glamorous cities—Rio de Janeiro.

A "city of beaches" is how many people describe Rio; there are 18 of them with romantic and exciting names like Flamingo and Botofogo, Copacobana and Ipanema, made famous by the song—"Tall and tanned and young and lovely, the girl from Ipanema goes walking, and when she walks each boy she passes goes 'wow'!"

The city rambles between dozens of sheer mountain peaks. Its most famous landmark is the gigantic statue of Christ, built on top of Corcovado mountain, and John headed straight there on our first morning.

It was 47 years ago when the people of Rio decided they wanted some kind of statue to welcome visitors to their city, so they called in architect Silva Costa. He named his statue "Christ the Redeemer" and built it out of granite and concrete. Its statistics are like something from the "Record Breakers"! It's 30 metres from head to toe, weighs 1450 tons, and took five years to construct. You really have to admire the men who built the statue—just getting the tools and equipment up Corcovado must have been terribly hard work. Corcovado's known locally as the "hunchback". It towers over the city—you can see it from almost anywhere. You drive most of the way up the mountain, but to reach the 709-metre summit

To the summit of Sugar Loaf mountain by cable car.

11

there's a climb of 227 steps. Tourists flock there in their thousands—not just to see the statue but also for the view. You can see for miles, and way below is Rio's second most famous landmark—the Sugar Loaf mountain.

While John was climbing up Corcovado, Lesley was on her way up the Sugar Loaf. It was an easier ascent than John's though—by cable car—but even that had its drawbacks.

"Being suspended on a 5000-metre-long cable isn't my ideal form of transport—I was glad when the ride was over!" Lesley gasped when she reached the top. But it was worth the agony, because the view was quite sensational.

As well as mountain climbing, we went beachcombing. Everyday life in Rio revolves around the beach. People born in the city are called "caricocas" and they use the beach not just for sunbathing and swimming, but for keeping fit! From

Dressed to explore the Iguaçú Falls.

Copacobana is one of Rio's 18 beaches.

dawn to dusk, men, women and children of all ages, shapes and sizes run, trot, jog, walk, and exercise by themselves or in groups, along the whole 6-kilometre length of Copacabana beach. There are also volley ball, beach tennis and 23 full-size football pitches.

Brazilians are football fanatics. Everywhere we went we saw a game being played. Whenever there's a big match on, the shops close early so that people can go to support their team. A big stadium's needed to accommodate all these fans, and they've got one. It's called "Maracana", and it's quite simply the biggest stadium in the world. Over 180,000 people can sit in comfort to watch the game. The players have huge dressing-rooms with individually piped oxygen and practice areas that are temperature controlled so that they're exactly the same temperature as the pitch outside. When you see the tremendous facilities, it's not surprising that Brazil has won the World Cup three times!

Brazil's so vast—you could put all the countries of Europe inside it and still have room to spare! Because it's so big, we decided to split up and explore different regions. John flew north-west to the hot, sticky jungles of Amazonia. Lesley went up the coast from Rio to Salvador, and then on to Brasilia—the country's space age capital—and Peter travelled south to the Rio Grande do Sul. This is the land of the Brazilian cowboys—the gauchos. At the Santa Barbara ranch he

Rio's statue of Christ the Redeemer—one of the world's most famous landmarks.

was given a real gaucho outfit to wear, and spent a day helping with the cattle rounde-up. Rio Grande do Sul is Brazil's main beef-producing area with over 25 million head of cattle.

The gauchos used to be nomads, wandering all over this part of South America. Nowadays they've settled down to become farmers, but they're determined to keep their age-old traditions alive. One of them is the "churrasco". It's a barbecue—but not quite like those at home. For one thing, the meat comes in rather large pieces—for a Brazilian, a kilo of beef is an average portion!

A gaucho churrasco—beef by the kilo! Brazil's cowboys round up over 25 million cattle.

The meat is pulled on to 2-metre-long stakes before being roasted on an open fire. 40 kilos were cooked for Pete's churrasco and it took a couple of hours to roast. After his first mouthful, Pete's verdict was: "Fatty and tough but it had a flavour all of its own!" Gauchos don't eat vegetables with their beef—but they wash it down with gaucho tea. It's called 'maté' and they make it by pouring hot water into the gourd full of green leaves. After letting it brew for a couple of minutes you drink it through a silver straw. It tastes like herb tea—not unpleasant, just unusual.

Another drink in Brazil is a lot more famous. As the song goes—"There's an awful lot of coffee in Brazil"—and while Pete was in the south, he visited a coffee farm.

The coffee bushes were only around a metre tall, and that's why the price of coffee rocketed a couple of years ago—those bushes should have been trees. In 1976, there was a very severe frost which killed off half the coffee trees in Brazil. Coffee beans became scarce and as new plants take years to mature, it's continued to be quite an expensive time for coffee drinkers.

After the beans have been picked, they have to be quality tested. At the Brazilian Coffee Institute, Peter met Julio Cesar Alves Pinto, one of the country's top coffee graders—and the way he graded the coffee

came as quite a shock. He took a cup of coffee—sucked a teaspoon of it into his mouth with the noisiest slurp you've ever heard—and then spat it out! Peter tried slurping for himself, and found it difficult keeping a straight face. It's a comic sight to see soberly-dressed businessmen making such disgusting noises! Julio told him that he can test twenty-nine cups of coffee every thirty seconds and that without a good slurp, you don't get the full flavour! It must work, too, because everywhere we went in Brazil, the coffee was superb!

To give you an idea of the vastness of the country, the coffee farm was as far away from John in Amazonia as London is from Istanbul.

It was a lot hotter too. This is the sweaty tropics—home of the mighty River Amazon. One fifth of the world's river water flows down the Amazon. It pours enough into the Atlantic Ocean every hour to keep a city the size of London supplied with water for five years. And there are so many different kinds of plant life that when a Brazilian botanist decided to catalogue them, he had to give up after counting a thousand plants in a single square mile!

In the middle of the jungle, a thousand miles from the coast, is the city of Manaus. Eighty years ago it was one of the richest cities on earth, rivalling those in Europe. The reason for its wealth was a tree—Hevea Brasiliensis—better known as the rubber tree. The rubber boom made many fortunes. But it didn't last. When the British-owned plantations in the Far East began producing rubber (from seedlings smuggled out of Brazil!) the Brazilians lost all their orders, their rubber wasn't as good, and was far more expensive. The city of Manaus became a ghost town and it remained one for around fifty years. But today, Manaus is booming again. It's a tax-free port so tourists flock there to buy cheap watches, radios, cameras and clothes. Fortunately, some of the old buildings still exist. The most famous is the Opera House, which, in its heyday, was used by the world's top artistes. Caruso, Pavlova and Nellie Melba were

The Opera House, Manaus—an early 1900 masterpiece in the heart of the jungle.

all brought there to perform. They couldn't fly into Manaus' supersonic airport either—for them it was a five-day journey by boat up the Amazon. They must have been a brave bunch of people because there was little protection from tropical diseases. One company who played there was struck down by yellow fever and out of eighty performers only eight survived!

It was quite eery inside the Opera House. You felt you could have been in a theatre in London, Paris or Rome—except for the oppressive heat! But it's undoubtedly one of the most beautiful theatres in the world.

It was in the state of Parana that we saw Brazil's most awe-inspiring spectacle—the Iguaçú Falls. You have to dress up in waterproofs and sou'westers to go near the falls. The air is so full of spray that without the special clothes, you'd get soaked to the skin. If you're brave, you can venture on the flimsy-looking walkways, built out over the falls, and watch the staggering sight of a million gallons of water a second pouring underneath your feet. But for an even more sensational view, helicopters take visitors for a bird's-eye view of the cascades. The pilots fly incredibly close to the thundering water.

"It felt as though we could have leant out and touched the water, it was one of those sights that literally makes you breathless!" said John as he climbed out of the chopper.

But the biggest sound of all in Brazil is the samba. It's played everywhere and its rhythm is so infectious you instinctively begin to tap your feet. In Salvador we were roped into dancing a Roda da Samba. It's a Brazilian knees-up—wherever there's a band and a crowd, a Roda da Samba is likely to begin. One by one, people are drawn into the centre of a circle and have to improvise a dance. Lesley did the samba with a man who kept spinning on his head, and John danced with a very large lady who had him literally on his knees!

In Rio, there's a different kind of samba. During July, it was the "middle year" samba; in February it's "Carnival Samba". The Rio Carnival is world famous; for three days the city goes samba mad.

There are five major samba schools, each with over 4000 pupils. These dances and musicians are called "sambistas" and Brazilians join and support a school like we support our football teams. Each school competes against the others at carnival time to win the top prize for the best costumes and, of course, the best samba.

Every year new dance steps have to be learnt, and even though carnival was still over six months away, the samba schools were already working on the next carnival samba. We joined one of the schools and they gave us their latest carnival costumes to wear. John's was all velvet and braid and 'extremely hot'! Lesley's was on the scanty side, ideal for non-stop sambaing in a hot climate.

At carnival, we were told, you'll find the streets are full of people dancing at any time of the day or night. We're not surprised you can't help dancing to that rhythm and now whenever we hear a samba being played, it brings back memories of all the amazing things we saw on our Expedition to Brazil.

14

It's Carnival time!

Roda da Samba—a dance with a difference—anything goes!

Face to Face

John meets himself at the world-famous Madame Tussaud's Waxworks Museum.

As soon as it became known that Madame Tussaud's was going to make a wax model of Shep and me, the joke went round the Blue Peter office that I was bound to be put in the Chamber of Horrors!

I wondered myself where they'd put me. Next to Muhammad Ali? I hoped not—he'd make me look a weed; then why not next to Napoleon—I'm about his size. But I didn't think I'd be happy there either. In the end, they decided I'd be put next to Percy Thrower—at least we wouldn't need any introduction!

Being modelled by Madame Tussaud's is quite an honour, so when Shep and I turned up there on a cold January morning, we were both a bit nervous. We were met by sculptors, Ian Hanson, who was going to work on me, and April Wilson, who was going to model Shep.

Ian began by measuring my head—from scalp to chin, ear to ear, mouth to chin, nose to chin, eyes to chin—dozens of measurements to make sure Ian's

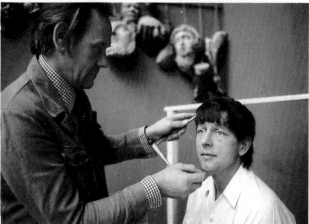

Sculptor Ian Hanson took dozens of measurements of my head to make sure the finished model was a perfect replica of me.

final wax model would be a perfect replica of me.

By my side, April measured up Shep. Every measurement had to be checked several times and I was very proud of Shep—he sat and stayed, and behaved like the perfect artist's model. The studio was full of other well-known people's heads and at times I had the distinct impression we were being watched!

We had dozens of photographs taken from all sorts of angles. This was so that Ian and April could carry on working after we'd gone home.

My eyes came in for special treatment. Ian produced a box full of glass eyeballs! My eyes are blue—but Ian had over 400 different types of blue eyes—some big, some small. He kept picking out one at a time and matching them with mine, until he found the perfect colour.

My head was sculpted in clay first so that a mould could be made, which would eventually produce the final cast in wax.

My hands came in for a different treatment. To save having to sculpt them, Ian took a plaster cast. I had to stand in the position of the finished model and plaster of paris was painted on my hands. To make sure Ian got a perfect mould, I had to keep very still even when I wanted to scratch my nose! When the plaster had set, it was very carefully chipped away with a hammer and chisel. Eventually, wax would be poured in, and out would come a replica of the Noakes hands.

Modelling people in wax dates back to before the days of the Pharaohs. You can see waxwork funeral effigies of kings and queens of England in Westminster Abbey. But it wasn't until Madame Tussaud arrived in Britain with her touring exhibition of famous people in 1802 that waxwork models became all the rage. The Duke of Wellington, King George IV and Sir Walter Scott were amongst her early successes.

Madame Tussaud began to learn her skills when she was just six years old. Little Anne-Marie was sent from her home in Strasbourg to live in Paris with her uncle, Dr Curtis, who was a famous modeller in wax. She, too, learned. . . . When she was 19, she was commanded to go and live in the Palace of Versailles to teach the King's sister how to make wax miniatures.

When the French Revolution broke out, Anne-Marie was imprisoned and forced to make death masks of her Royalist friends. It must have been a ghastly time, but the fact she was so talented probably saved her life.

For 33 years, Madame Tussaud toured Great Britain with her travelling show and it wasn't until she was 74 that a permanent home was found for the exhibition—in London's Marylebone Road—and it's stayed there ever since.

It took over four months to complete our models then we went back to help put ourselves on show!

Coming face to face with yourself is quite a shock. Make-up artist Vera Bland was just finishing off my head. The hair had been put in one hair at a time and dyed to match mine. Cathy Holton cut and styled it into the unique Noakes shape.

Shep had been made of fibreglass and looked incredibly lifelike. He's the first dog ever to be modelled by Madame Tussaud's. When he saw the model for the first time, I don't think he recognised himself—if he did, he didn't react at all! Perhaps he was too surprised—and I can't say I blame him

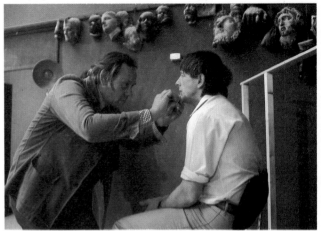

Dozens of famous "heads" gazed down as I was measured.

Shep was the first dog ever to be modelled at Madame Tussaud's.

A plaster cast was made of my hands.

"Eye, eye!" Ian matched mine from 400 spares.

And each one a perfect match.

Percy Thrower didn't seem too interested in his new neighbour.

Putting my head on my body was a peculiar moment.

because it really is very peculiar seeing a full-size, amazingly lifelike model of yourself, correct in every detail—even in my case down to the Blue Peter badge.

Ian asked if I'd help carry myself into the exhibition, so with my head tucked underneath my arm I walked past some very surprised tourists—not to mention film star Audrey Hepburn, jockey Lester Piggott, and footballer Kevin Keegan—until we reached Percy Thrower. That's where I was put, with fibreglass Shep at my feet. I don't know how long we'll be there, but I shouldn't think it'll be as long as Nelson!

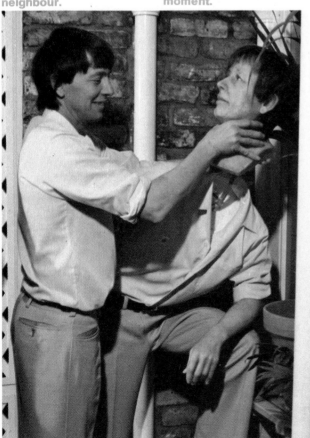

Which ones are the real John Noakes and Shep?

SOUPER SPUD!

Bangers and Mash, Fish and Chips, Shepherd's Pie . . . where would these great British dishes be without the good old potato?

Potatoes are so much part of our everyday life it's difficult to imagine what it would be like without them. . . .

1 . . . But for hundreds of years, potatoes were unknown in Britain. Ordinary people ate coarse bread, or a kind of porridge, with a bit of salt meat if they were lucky.

2 Then the Spaniards went to South America. In the markets of Peru, they saw strange, brown, knobbly things. "We call them battata," said the people. "Are they stones or fruit?" asked the Spaniards.

3 So they were shown plants growing in the fields, and processions of priests in fantastic robes calling on their gods to bless the crop.

4 A monk from Spain, called Hieronymous Carden, picked up some of the strange objects and put them in his pouch, trying to remember their name. "Potato!" he muttered.

5 And back in Spain he planted them in the garden of his monastery. They were the first potatoes ever grown in Europe.

6 In England, Queen Elizabeth I was given some potatoes brought back from the New World by the great voyagers, Hawkins and Drake.

7 A botanist called John Gerade wrote a book called a "Herbal", and he described the new plant: "Some of the potatoes are round as a ball, some oval or egg fashion with knobbly roots fastened unto the stalks with infinite number of thready string"—which is really quite a good description of a potato plant.

8 Soon people began to grow potatoes in their herb gardens—as a medicine! A slice of potato in the pocket was supposed to be a splendid remedy for rheumatism, but hardly anyone actually ate them.

9 Then in France, a landowner called Antoine Parmentier grew great fields of potatoes and called in important Government officials to see them. "Look," he said, "loads of food, all underground, quite safe! It can't be ruined by storm, and in war, even armies marching over the fields can't destroy the potatoes."

10 Parmentier and his chef invented a soup called Potage à la Parmentier, to persuade people how delicious potatoes were to eat.

11 Parmentier even went to court and persuaded the King of France, Louis XVI, to wear a spray of potato flowers in his buttonhole. Potatoes had arrived in France!

12 After Parmentier died, the French people were so grateful to him that every year they planted potatoes on his grave in memory of him.

19

13 But Englishmen still despised potatoes and only wanted to eat meat and bread. "Fruit breeds fevers, and potatoes are an unworthy substitute for bread," many a true-born Englishman declared.

14 The Emperor Napoleon of France changed all that, however. He made plans to invade England. "I will starve the people of Britain and force them to surrender," he declared.

15 In London, a Board of Agriculture was formed to help grow more food and they decided on growing potatoes.

16 So at last in Britain, nearly 300 years after potatoes had first reached Europe, farms were growing potatoes everywhere.

17 And soon they were so cheap, everyone could afford them. For many poor families, potatoes were their only hot food from one week to the next.

18 New, delicious ways were invented for cooking them. One of the favourites was sold by the baked potato men, people queued by their barrows, children bought the potatoes, and gentlemen would buy them for ladies to hold inside their muffs to keep their hands warm. However you used them, potatoes were here to stay!

Monsieur Parmentier died 165 years ago—but his famous soup lives on! If you're having a party on bonfire night, why not make it for your friends? It's tasty, filling and *easy*.

Potage à la Parmentier

For 4 people you will need:
500g. peeled potatoes (chopped into very thin slices)
1 medium-sized onion (also cut into thin slices)
40g. butter
1 bayleaf
575ml. milk
250ml. water
Salt and pepper to taste
Parsley and croûtons for garnish.

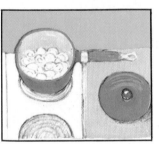

2 Cook for about 5 minutes on a *very low heat* until the potatoes and onions are soft, but *still white*. This is very important.

3 Add the milk, water, bayleaf and seasoning. Stir and bring *slowly* to the boil. Then let the soup simmer very gently for about 20 minutes (with the mixture just bubbling at the edges).

4 Remove the bayleaf and get rid of the lumps of vegetables by pouring through a sieve and squashing the lumps with a wooden spoon or mixing in a blender.

1 Melt the butter in a saucepan and add the chopped potatoes and onions. Give them a quick stir and put a lid on the saucepan to keep in the heat.

5 Heat before serving, and for a finishing touch add some croûtons—little squares of stale bread, fried until they're golden brown with a sprinkling of salt.

FIT FOR A QUEEN

If you were made a life peer in the Queen's Birthday or New Year Honours lists, you'd need a set of robes to take your seat in the House of Lords. Most new peers and peeresses rent them for the occasion because a brand-new set of robes can cost several thousand pounds.

During the Queen's Jubilee year, there were many special ceremonial occasions where robes had to be worn and for one shop in Chancery Lane in London, it was a bumper year. "Ede and Ravenscroft" have been making ceremonial robes for 300 years. They've had "By Appointment" warrants as robe makers for the last 13 Kings and Queens. And as well as royalty, their famous clients have included Admiral Lord Nelson and Sir Winston Churchill.

Mr John Clark, the managing director, showed us records of all their transactions and explained that the ancient books are kept for a very good reason. When a University or Council wants a new robe designed, they consult Ede and Ravenscroft who, by checking their records, can make sure the new design will be completely original and not a copy of someone else's. They are now recognised as the world authority.

We met Mrs Batteson in the sewing room. She was busy putting together a robe for a Nigerian University.

The real gold thread used for the embroidered designs costs £10.00 per ounce.

Master of the Rolls.

Ph.D. robes—University of Strathclyde.

A Beadle's robe.

A Herald's tabard.

Mrs Batteson showed me a newly-commissioned robe for a University in Nigeria.

It was splendidly ornate in red, purple and lots of gold. As she said, "they like a lot of bright colours and ornaments."

Many foreign countries' governments and universities come to London for their robes and don't seem to mind paying the thousands of pounds they cost. One of the reasons they're so expensive is that they're decorated with the highest quality materials, like gold thread. The gold is in very small "tubes". and we watched embroiderer Joan Phillips thread the tubes on to a needle and stitch them in place. She was decorating a rather grand medieval castle that was growing grander with each piece of gold thread.

Ede and Ravenscroft don't just make robes for occasional ceremonial use—but ones for everyday use, worn by judges and barristers in courts, complete with wigs made of horse-hair.

It's not every day you get the chance of dressing up as a Queen's herald or a Beadle, so when we were given the freedom of the stock room, we went

The Most Noble Order of the Garter.

Viscount Noakes of Halifax and Viscountess Judd of Shepherd's Bush take a ride down the Mall.

wild and tried on as many different outfits as we could.

The grandest were the ermine-trimmed scarlet robes and coronets of a Viscount and Viscountess.

With just a hint of a smile, the staff of Ede and Ravenscroft bowed the Viscount Noakes of Halifax and Viscountess Judd of Shepherd's Bush out of the shop as we took to the streets of London in an open carriage. We did it for a bit of a giggle, but all the tourists grabbed their cameras and our ride down the Mall must be one of the most recorded events of the year. We often wonder exactly *who* the tourists thought we were—and what they told their friends and relations when they got back home?

You've run out of pocket money and can't afford to buy presents? Fear not—these Handy Holders are the answer! Nine small wooden clothes pegs will transform one old yogurt pot into a present to be proud of. Here's the secret:

HANDY HOLDERS

Small Holder

1 Wash an empty yogurt pot and paint inside *and* out with enamel paint.
2 Take the springs from nine wooden clothes pegs by twisting the two wooden parts in opposite directions.
3 Glue the half clothes pegs to the pot; keeping the smooth tapering ends of each peg at the bottom and spacing the pegs a little apart at the top. After glueing about four or five pegs, leave them to dry, then continue until the whole pot is covered. When all the pegs are glued on, gently sandpaper them smooth and paint with clear varnish.
4 To make a top, use a lid from a cream cheese container, paint it with the enamel paint and cover the centre part with sticky-backed plastic.

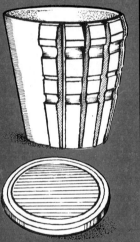

Tray Holder

Cut off the bottom part of a soap-powder packet and cover with pegs glued close together—leaving no spaces.

Tall Holder

1 Cut off the bottom of a washing-up liquid container and paint inside and out.
2 Glue a circle of pegs around the bottom of the container with the *flat smooth end* of the peg at the *top*.
3 Glue a second circle of pegs around the top of the pot, with the flat smooth ends of the pegs *downwards*, overlapping the top of the first circle and allowing the top of the pegs to stand above the top of the container.

10 CM

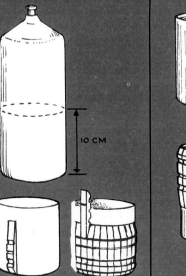

Tin Holder with Lid
(Useful for biscuits)

1 Paint the outside of a dried milk tin and glue a circle of pegs around the *top* of the tin.
2 Overlap with a bottom circle of pegs below the bottom of the tin.
3 Cover the middle of the tin's lid with sticky-backed plastic. Make a hole in the middle of the lid and fix a saucepan lid handle. Paint handle with enamel paint.

25

HOW I JOINED BLUE PETER

For the first week after I heard that I'd got the job, I used to wake up in the middle of the night and think it was all a dream. I suppose it's not surprising really, because I had the phone call from the Blue Peter office at 10 o'clock in the morning—and as I'd been working in a disco until 2.00 a.m., I was only semi-conscious when I heard the news.

"How did you manage to get a marvellous job like that?" all my friends asked when I told them. I was tempted to say it was because I'm so handsome and talented—but I decided to settle for the truth.

"It's because I'm so lucky," I said.

It all started back home on my father's farm at Dethick in Derbyshire. Gem, our border collie, and I had just got the cows into the parlour to start milking when my Dad popped his head round the door.

"The BBC is coming here to film next week," he said.

I was interested, because although I've always helped my father on the farm when I've been home, it's never been my regular job. After I left University, I worked as a teacher for 18 months at Long Eaton School. I enjoyed it very much, but ever since I was at school myself, I've had a hankering to get into broadcasting. And so one day I chucked it all up

and went to be a disc jockey in Germany!

Being a D.J. looks like a doddle of a job—just putting on records and chatting. But like a lot of other things which seem relaxed and easy, there's a lot of hard work involved to give the audience the impression that you've just strolled in to play your favourite records. I had a great time and learned a lot during my ten months in Cologne. In the summer of 1977, I came back home to the farm before I started a new job at a London disco. It was then that the BBC film crew arrived.

They were shooting a six-part serial called *A Traveller in Time*. It was about a girl who visits her relatives in a Tudor farmhouse and slips back in time to the days of Mary, Queen of Scots. Our farm made an ideal location because parts of the house are more than 600 years old. I was fascinated by the filming. The girl, played by 15-year-old Sophie Thompson, was clearly giving a brilliant performance. But it was the studio concentration and the dynamic energy of the Director that amazed me. Dorothea Brooking has been a top Children's Director for more than thirty years. She was twice as old as some of the crew, and yet at the end of a long day, when everyone else was beginning to flag, Dorothea seemed to have energy to spare. I was looking for interesting people to interview for a job I was hoping to do for a local radio station, so I plucked up my courage and asked Dorothea.

Interviewing TV director Dorothea Brooking was my lucky break.

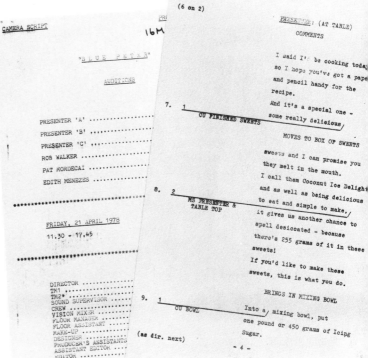

CAMERA SCRIPT

"BLUE PETER"

AUDITIONS

PRESENTER 'A' ....
PRESENTER 'B' ....
PRESENTER 'C' ....
ROB WALKER ....
PAT MORDECAI ....
EDITH MENEZES ....

FRIDAY, 21 APRIL 1978

11.30 – 17.45

DIRECTOR ....
TM1 ....
TM2* ....
SOUND SUPERVISOR ....
CREW ....
VISION MIXER ....
FLOOR MANAGER ....
FLOOR ASSISTANT ....
MAKE-UP ....
DESIGNER ....
PRODUCER'S ASSISTANTS
ASSISTANT EDITOR ....
EDITOR ....   (as dir. next)

(6 on 2)

PRESENTER: (AT TABLE)
COMMENTS

I said I'd be cooking today, so I hope you've got a paper and pencil handy for the recipe.

7.   1   And it's a special one – some really delicious
CU FINISHED SWEETS

                           MOVES TO BOX OF SWEETS

                           sweets and I can promise you they melt in the mouth.
8.   2   I call them Coconut Ice Delight
MS PRESENTER &   and as well as being delicious
TABLE TOP   to eat and simple to make,
                           it gives us another chance to spell desiccated – because there's 255 grams of it in these sweets!

                           If you'd like to make these sweets, this is what you do.

                           BRINGS IN MIXING BOWL

9.   1   Into a mixing bowl, put
      CU BOWL   one pound or 450 grams of Icing Sugar.

                           - 4 -

My Blue Peter audition script. Edward Barnes told me to learn it overnight.

That interview (although it never actually went out on the air!) was my lucky break. The following week, Dorothea met Edward Barnes, the Deputy Head of Children's Programmes, who happened to tell her that they were looking for a new man for Blue Peter—and she said "Why don't you see Simon Groom?" Of course, *I* knew nothing about this until I had a phone call at 10 o'clock one morning (yes, I was asleep again) asking me if I would come to the Television Centre to see Edward Barnes that afternoon.

After about ten minutes' chat about Blue Peter, he got up and left the office saying he'd be back in a minute. He came back holding a thick, yellow audition script.

"Learn that and come back here at 7 o'clock tomorrow night," he said.

Needless to say, I'd never seen a television script before—and I didn't know what half the camera instructions on the left-hand side of the page were about. But I decided that was someone else's worry, and concentrated on getting the rest of the script into my head.

It was like a mini Blue Peter. I had to do an item about Jack and Jill going to a cat show—then make some sweets—and finish up doing an interview whilst bouncing up and down on a trampoline!

I arrived at 7 o'clock at Main Reception at the Television Centre to be met by Biddy Baxter in person. She was very friendly, and kept telling me not to be nervous. She needn't have bothered—I wasn't nervous—I was terrified!

Pat Mordecai, one of the Blue Peter directors, was pretending to be either Lesley or John, so that I had someone to chat to. I had the real cats, although they didn't stick around for long, and a real trampolinist to interview.

And that was my undoing!

Everything went reasonably well until I started to try out the trampoline exercises.

"Now jump and bring your knees up—then sit down on the trampoline," said Rob Walker, the trampolinist.

"Is that called a touch up?" I asked.

"A touch up?" said Rob, incredulously. (I thought it didn't sound quite right, but this was no time to hesitate.)

"Yes," I said, confidently.

"You mean a 'tuck jump'," he said. The whole studio fell about with laughter—and I felt absolutely terrible.

Biddy came down on the floor and said I'd done very well, and not to worry about the "touch up"—and they'd be letting me know in about a week's time.

I really thought I'd blown it, and I tried to put the whole thing out of my head.

Then, on a damp, April morning, the phone bell brought me back to consciousness and I heard Biddy Baxter saying, "Congratulations! You've just joined the Blue Peter team."

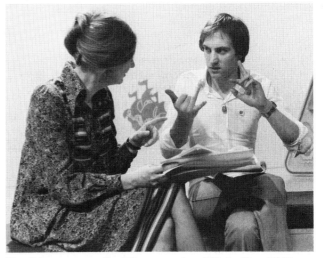
Next day was my first time ever in a TV studio—Biddy Baxter put me at my ease.

DO YOU HAVE A PROBLEM?

**Can you multiply
637432 × 513124
in your head?**

Mrs Shakuntala Devi can, and proved it when she came to the studio (the answer is 327081657568). She also found the cube root of 71991296 in two seconds flat (416) and gave the dates of every Sunday in 1978—that took her precisely thirty seconds. And when we asked her what day 31 May 1951 was, she replied instantly—Thursday. An extraordinary lady!

If Mrs Shakuntala Devi's calculations are a bit too hard for you, try this and amaze your friends by guessing their birthdays!

Guess your friend's birthday

Tell your friends to work out the number of the month they were born in:

1 January	7 July
2 February	8 August
3 March	9 September
4 April	10 October
5 May	11 November
6 June	12 December

Ask them to multiply the number of the month by five, add six to the total and multiply that answer by 4. Now add 9 and multiply by 5. This grand total must have the date of their birth added to it.
Example: Lesley's birthday is 20 December. December is the 12th month, so 12×5= 60.
Add 6= 66; multiply by 4= 264; add 9= 273; multiply by 5= 1365; add date of birth 1365+ 20= 1385
Now comes the magic. Ask your friends for their final total. All you have to do is subtract 165. From the answer the last two digits give you the date of the month, and the first one or two the number of the month. In Lesley's case, 1385− 165= 1220. Month of birth 12; 20 date of birth. Her birthday is 20 December!

PADDINGTON PASSES THROUGH

STORY BY MICHAEL BOND

ILLUSTRATED BY "HARGREAVES"

The Commissionaire on duty outside the B.B.C. Television Centre gazed doubtfully at the small figure standing in front of him.

"It's all highly irregular," he said. "By rights you should either have a pass issued by someone in authority, or . . ." he made a stabbing motion with his forefinger in the direction of the main building, **"*or*, I'm supposed to telephone the person or persons concerned in order to check your bona fides. For all I know," he added darkly, "they may not be quite what they're cracked up to be."**

Paddington gave the man a hard stare. "My bona fides are cracked!" he exclaimed in alarm.

The Commissionaire sighed. He was practically at the end of his period of duty and he had no wish to mar what had been an otherwise calm and trouble free day by getting himself involved in a complicated discussion on the subject of bears' credentials.

"On the other hand," he continued hastily, "seeing as I know you by sight from your previous visits, and seeing as it's Friday and most of the office staff have gone home by now, I reckon I could take a chance." He eyed Paddington through the gathering dusk. "I take it you do have some means of identification—just for the record?"

Paddington opened his suitcase and peered inside. "There's a photograph of my Aunt Lucy," he said. "No one else has got one like that." He held it

up for the man to see and then rummaged around still further. "Or there's this. It's got my paw mark on it."

The Commissionaire gave a shudder as Paddington held up the squashed remains of a marmalade sandwich. "I don't suppose anyone else has got one like that either," he said with feeling.

Convinced beyond all shadow of doubt of his visitor's identity, the man disappeared inside his box and after consulting a list pinned to the wall came out again and handed Paddington a piece of paper with a figure written on it.

"That's the number of the studio you want," he said, as he raised the barrier. "You can leave your things there overnight, but mind you come straight out again . . . and no touching anything."

Paddington returned the man's salute with a grateful raising of his hat. Then he picked up his suitcase with one paw and grasped the handle of his shopping basket on wheels with the other.

It took him a moment or two to get going as the basket was, to say the very least, somewhat

29

overladen. Over the years it had stood Paddington, not to mention the rest of the Brown family, in good stead fetching and carrying the weekly shopping between the Portobello Road and Windsor Gardens, but it was safe to say that during all that time it had probably never been quite so full.

It was piled high with an assortment of items ranging from mysterious packets tied up with string, through boxes of games and other pieces of bric-a-brac, to an old guitar which was perched precariously on top.

It overflowed to such an extent Paddington found it difficult to see where he was going let alone where he had been, and on his way across the forecourt he had to stop several times in order to mop his brow. In doing so he somehow or other missed the main entrance to the Television Centre, and when he eventually stopped to check his whereabouts he found to his surprise that he had ended up outside some large doors at the back of the building.

Paddington was familiar with the layout of the B.B.C. studios, and from past experience he remembered that these doors led straight into a wide circular corridor which ran round the outside of the building and was used to feed the different studios with scenery and other equipment.

As he came to a halt one of the doors slid back and a small electric trolley poked its nose out. It was towing a line of longer trucks laden with scenery, and as it slowed down to turn the corner the driver caught sight of Paddington and came to a halt alongside him.

"Can I help you, mate?" he called.

Paddington held his piece of paper up for the man to see. "I was looking for this studio," he announced.

The man gave it a brief glance and then took in Paddington's shopping basket on wheels. "Along there, second door on the left," he said, pointing along the corridor. "But you'd better hurry. The red light's flashing so they must be about to start. If I were you I'd leave your stuff just inside the door 'ere, grab your guitar and run."

"They're about to have a jam session," called another man, who was helping load some scenery onto a second truck.

"A jam session?" Paddington licked his lips as he propped his basket against the wall where the first man had suggested. "If I'd known, I'd have brought a sliced loaf with me."

The driver scratched his head as Paddington hurried off up the corridor clutching his guitar. "Rum lot these folk singers," he said. "Talk a language all their own."

"A good shave wouldn't do some of 'em any harm," agreed the second man in a loud voice.

But if he was trying to make any sort of point he was wasting his time, for Paddington was already disappearing through the door leading to the studio. There was a momentary blast of music and then, as the door swung shut behind him, the red light which had been winking furiously beforehand glowed steadily to show that the programme was on the air.

Once inside, Paddington picked his way across a maze of cables and round several lots of scenery, until he finally found himself standing near a stage alongside two men, one of whom was wearing headphones. A few feet away another man in evening dress was poised on a rostrum before a group of musicians.

As Paddington arrived the man brought the music to an end with a wave of his hand and then stepped down and beckoned towards the wings.

"Ladies and gentlemen," he announced, as the cameras and microphone boom moved in, "this *is* Sonny Climes speaking. Now, I would like to present my first guest of the evening . . ."

Feeling most surprised Paddington pushed his way past the two men and hurried across the studio.

He raised his hat several times in the direction of some applause which rose from the darkness beyond and then held out his paw.

"Good evening, Mr Climes," he said. "I've come about the jam."

Sonny Climes' jaw, which had dropped more than somewhat on catching sight of Paddington, now fell even further. "You've come about the jam?" he repeated. "What jam?"

In asking Paddington about the jam, Sonny Climes made it sound as if it was only the first of many questions hovering on his lips, and that finding other things to ask was likely to be the least of his problems. But certainly, had he suffered any kind of shortage he could have found eager and willing assistance from more than one person only a short bus ride away.

Back at number thirty-two Windsor Gardens the Browns gazed in horror at their television receiver.

"Crumbs!" exclaimed Jonathan. "Paddington!"

It was an obvious remark to make, but one which needed saying if only to confirm the fact that they were all seeing the same picture on their screen.

"I knew we shouldn't have let that bear go off to the Television Centre by himself," said Mrs Bird. "Something always happens when he's left to his own devices."

"Ssh!" said Mr Brown. "I think the conductor is saying something."

Trying to make the best of a bad job, Sonny Climes sought in the dark recesses of his mind for a tune which might have something to do with jam and which would suit his unexpected guest.

"Do you by any chance know 'It must be jelly 'cause jam don't shake like that'?" he asked hopefully, as he gave a signal to the band.

There was a rustle of music as Paddington considered the matter for a moment. "Perhaps it's the heat from the lights," he said. "Some of Mrs Bird's marmalade goes very wobbly in the hot weather—especially the sort without many chunks in it."

The rustling of paper in the background grew more frantic.

"I don't think that's in our repertoire," said Mr Climes in a voice which was growing more and more high pitched. "But we could have a go. Is it in A Flat?"

It was Paddington's turn to look puzzled. "No," he said firmly. "It's at 32 Windsor Gardens."

Paddington was beginning to share in Mr Climes' unhappiness about the way things were going. Out of the corner of his eye he could just see the man with the headphones. He was waving his arms about in a way which made Magnus Pike look like a tailor's dummy, pointing first at the man standing beside him and then at the conductor.

"I think," announced Paddington, "I may go and get some sandwiches in the canteen instead, Mr Climes." And with that he turned on his heels and hurried off the set in the opposite direction to the way he'd come. He didn't like the expression on the studio manager's face at all, and he disappeared into the corridor as fast as his legs would carry him.

It was as he did so that he had his second shock of the evening; one, moreover, that caused him to stop dead in his tracks as if the whole world was about to collapse about his ears.

Only a few minutes before the corridor had been a hive of activity; now it was quiet and deserted, stripped bare of all the piles of scenery and props which had lined its walls.

But it wasn't the absence of scenery or those who'd been moving it that caused Paddington's alarm, it was the fact that his shopping basket on wheels had disappeared as well.

For a moment or two he gazed at the spot where it had been as if he could hardly believe his eyes, then he pulled himself together and a purposeful look came over his face; one which boded ill for anyone who got between him and his objective.

Unaware of the drama that was taking place, the Browns continued their council of war back at number thirty-two Windsor Gardens.

"What shall we do?" asked Mrs Brown.

"I don't see what we can do," said Mr Brown. "What's he doing there anyway?"

"Goodness only knows," said Mrs Brown. "He spent the morning rummaging about in the attic and that's usually a bad sign."

"Knowing that bear," said Mrs Bird, "I'm sure he'll tell us all about it in his own good time, and I'm equally sure there are those at this very moment who are quite capable of putting things to rights."

Mrs Bird spoke with a confidence she didn't entirely feel, and if the caption on their screen saying that 'normal service would be resumed as soon as possible' was anything to go by, the shock waves of Paddington's unexpected appearance were still reverberating around the Television Centre as well. Even the announcer seemed to have lost his usual calm and he apologised several times for putting on a record at the wrong speed.

"Perhaps we should try BBC 2?" suggested Jonathan. "It's the story of Samuel Pepys."

"Anything's better than this," agreed Mr Brown, as he got up to press the button.

Trying hard to dismiss the matter from their minds the Browns settled back in their chairs in an attempt to adjust themselves mentally to the change of programme.

They appeared to have tuned in at a fairly quiet moment in the play, for Mr Pepys was standing at a high desk near the window of his lodgings, clasping a quill pen in his hand while he gazed reflectively through some French windows leading to the garden outside.

"Methinks," he began. "Methinks I see . . ." Even as he began to speak Mr Pepys' eyes took on a slightly glazed look.

Unlike most programmes which were pre-recorded, the Samuel Pepys serial was going out live. It was all part of a plan to borrow from some of the more popular children's programmes like Blue Peter and inject some excitement into the series, but if the look on Mr Pepys' face at that moment was anything to go by he would have been perfectly happy to settle for a quiet recorded life.

He mopped his brow with a kerchief and with a trembling hand dipped his quill into the ink again. "Methinks," he repeated, "I saw a bear go past the window. It was wearing a duffle coat and an old hat and it was carrying some kind of suitcase. Perhaps," he said hopefully, turning to the camera, "it belonged to some strolling players and has gone on its way never to be seen again?''

But Mr Pepys hoped in vain. Before he had a chance to recharge his quill, let alone pen any more thoughts in his diary, there was a knock at the door, followed by a flurry of movement from the cameras as they changed position to take in this unexpected development.

''Good evening,'' said Paddington, raising his hat as he entered the room.

''Er . . . good morrow,'' said the luckless actor desperately. He gave a deep bow. ''Samuel Pepys. . . .''

''Does he really?'' said Paddington. He gave the man a hard stare. ''Mrs Bird says that's rude.''

''Er . . . Mistress Bird?'' said the actor desperately. ''Verily I do not think I know the wench.''

''*Wench!*'' repeated Paddington hotly. ''Mrs Bird isn't a wench!''

''Perhaps,'' said the man hastily as Paddington gave him another hard stare, ''perhaps I could read to you from my diary?''

Paddington considered the matter for a moment. ''It's very kind of you,'' he said at last. ''If I had the time I could read to you from my scrap-book as well. Only I'm in a hurry. I'm afraid I've lost something very important.''

''Oh, dear. Can I help you?'' asked Mr Pepys, clutching at straws.

''I don't think so,'' replied Paddington gloomily. He cast his eye round Mr Pepys' room. ''I don't think what I want has been invented yet!''

The babble of noise which emerged from the dozens of pairs of headphones being worn by the technicians in the studio was equalled only by the groan which rose from the living room at number thirty-two Windsor Gardens as they took in this latest piece of news.

''We *must* do something,'' said Mrs Brown. ''We can't just leave him there to his own devices. There's no knowing what he'll do next.''

Mrs Bird rose to her feet. ''I'm going to make some 'phone calls,'' she said. ''There's not much point in having friends in high places if you can't call on them in times of emergency.''

Mrs Bird hurried from the room. Through Paddington's many escapades in the past she had acquired quite a few telephone numbers, mostly those of the members of the *Blue Peter* team, and she felt sure they would be only too pleased to help in any way possible.

But on her return to the living room Mrs Bird's face looked, if anything, even longer than it had when she had left.

''Not a single reply,'' she said. ''They must all be out.''

''Well,'' said Mrs Brown, trying to strike a cheerful note. ''No news is good news.''

''Talking of which,'' said Mr Brown as he pressed a button on the television and some music burst forth, ''perhaps we could try watching the nine o'clock news. They may mention something on that.''

The music faded as a picture of Angela Rippon filled the screen, and with her customary air of calm

managed to convey the feeling that even if all was not entirely well with the world at large at least things were reasonably safe at the Television Centre. Once again the Browns settled back and found themselves lulled into a sense of security as the day's events unfolded before their eyes.

It was as she neared the end of the programme and began reciting the main points of the news again that Miss Rippon's eyes took on a slightly

glazed look. She shifted uneasily in her chair as a shadow fell across the scenery behind her, hovered for a moment, disappeared, then reappeared again.

''And that,'' she said quickly but firmly, ''is the end of the news.''

At the sound of her words the shadow sprang to life with a clearly visible raising of a hat. ''No it isn't!'' called a voice.

''Crikey!'' groaned Jonathan. ''Here he comes again!''

''Excuse me, Miss Rippon!'' cried Paddington hotly as he came into view. ''Before you finish the news I've got another main point. Someone's taken my shopping basket on wheels!''

Paddington looked as if he was about to address the nation at great length on the subject, but by now the engineers were more than ready for any emergency, and before he had a chance to say any more the picture faded from the screen.

''So that's it!'' exclaimed Judy. ''No wonder he's upset.''

''Only Paddington could lose a shopping basket on wheels in the Television Centre,'' said Jonathan. ''I wouldn't mind betting he'll put in a lot more appearances before the end of the evening,'' he added, trying to keep the note of hope from his voice.

Mrs Bird rose to her feet, ''Not if I have anything to do with it,'' she said grimly. ''I don't know what the rest of you are doing, but I'm off to the B.B.C.

*   *   *

The Director of the Evaluation of Audience Figures bounded out from behind his desk as Paddington entered the room closely followed by a throng of other people.

"Good evening," he said, holding out his hand. "I'm D.E.A.F."

"Oh, dear!" said Paddington. "I'm sorry about that." He rummaged for a moment or two in his newly recovered shopping basket on wheels and then withdrew a large metal funnel. "Perhaps you'd like to use this," he shouted at the top of his voice, as he placed the small end to his lips and directed the larger end towards the man's head. "It's an old one of Mrs Bird's, but it makes a very good ear trumpet."

John, Peter and Lesley exchanged glances with the Browns as the Director staggered back clutching his ear. They could sense the start of some complicated misunderstandings, and there had been enough of those already that evening. Enough, that is, to send all those present rushing post haste to the Television Centre in the hope of averting any more disasters.

John cupped a hand to his mouth. "He's not deaf," he hissed. "He's Dee Ee Aye Eff—that's not the same thing at all. People are always using initials at the B.B.C." He was about to add that they usually did so because it saved time, but catching sight of the expression on Paddington's face he decided that it might not always hold true.

"Perhaps you would like to tell us your story in your own words?" suggested the Director, addressing Paddington as he retired to the safety of his desk.

Paddington considered the matter for a moment. So much had happened that evening he wasn't quite sure where to begin. "Well," he said, "I'm P.B. and I come from D.P. I brought my S.B.O.W. to the B.B.C. because I wanted to be ready for the M.C.S.S. tomorrow."

If Paddington thought his explanation would help clear the air he was doomed to disappointment.

"Er . . . would you mind repeating that in plain language?" asked the Director.

Paddington gave the man a funny look. For someone who liked using initials he didn't seem to know much about them.

"I'm Paddington Brown," he explained patiently, "and I come from Darkest Peru. I brought my shopping basket on wheels to the B.B.C. and I left it in a corridor with some scenery while I went into a studio by mistake, and when I came out again it had gone, so I've been looking for it ever since."

Peter glanced at Paddington's basket. "If you left that out in the scenery corridor," he said, "no wonder it disappeared. They probably thought it was being used in GOING FOR A SONG."

"Going for a Song?" repeated Paddington hotly. "I was hoping to get more for it than that. It was meant for the M.C.S.S."

"The M.C.S.S.?" chorused everyone else.

"What's that when it's at home?" exclaimed Mr Brown.

Paddington gave a deep sigh. He was beginning to wish people would make up their minds exactly what they *did* want from him. One moment it was initials, the next moment it wasn't.

"M.C.S.S. is the Multi Coloured Swap Shop," he explained patiently. "I had rather a lot of things to swap so I thought I would bring them along the night before just to make sure. The man at the gate gave me a piece of paper with the number of the studio on. It was studio 6, only I must have held it upside down by mistake because I was shown into number 9."

The silence which greeted Paddington's latest announcement was broken by Mrs Brown. "I'm very sorry about all this," she exclaimed, turning to the Director. "We had no idea. . . ."

"Sorry?" repeated the Director of Audience Figures. "My dear lady, there's no need to be sorry." He jumped to his feet again. "Why, it's the best thing that's happened to me in years. The reason I asked you all up here is so that I can congratulate this young bear personally. Since he arrived at the studios we've been flooded with reports from all over the country about people tuning in to see when and where he's going to appear next. Word gets around you know. Why, the news got a bigger audience than the World Cup, and we've had a lot of complaints because we faded it."

He turned back to Paddington and looked at him wistfully. "I wish we could find a way of fitting you into our schedules every night of the year," he exclaimed. "It would probably mean promotion."

"I could start now if you like," said Paddington eagerly. "It's quite easy really. All you do is go in through doors. If I hurry I might be in time for *Sky at Night.*"

"Er, yes," said the Director hastily. "On the other hand, there's a lot to be said for keeping people guessing and enough's as good as a feast. Talking of which, I wonder if you would all care to join me in a little something before we turn in? I daresay you could do with some refreshment."

"A marmalade sandwich?" suggested John, giving the others a wink.

"Followed by a nice cup of hot cocoa?" added Lesley.

"You'll need building up if you're going to be on the M.C.S.S. tomorrow morning," agreed Peter. "It starts early."

Paddington considered the matter for a moment. What with one thing and another it *had* been a busy time and he was feeling very hungry.

"I think," he announced to everyone's relief, "that's a very good idea. There's nothing like rounding things off with a M.S. and a C.O.H.C. before you go to B. Especially," he added, gazing around all his friends, "when you can share it with F's like J.P. and Miss J. from B.P., not to mention all the B's from W.G.!"

The next time you watch Blue Peter, try this experiment: cover your ears until all the sound is muffled, then imagine what it would be like to hear strange, high-pitched, sizzling noises—or low, booming thuds—while you were looking at us doing the programme.

You'd think you were in the middle of some kind of dreadful nightmare, but that's what life is like *all the time* for many of the one in every four hundred children in Britain, who are either completely deaf or very hard of hearing.

The more we found out about the problems deaf children battle with, the more we wanted to help. As John said:

"At least if you become deaf when you're grown up, you keep all your knowledge of words and how to use them—even if you can't hear them any more. But if you're *born* deaf, how do you ever start to learn things in the first place?"

One way, we discovered, is by being able to use very special equipment that lights up to tell deaf people whether or not they're making the right noises when they're learning to speak.

It's used in most of Britain's eighty schools for deaf children. But the problem is, that the schools can only help a fraction of the children in need. The rest have to go to ordinary schools where it can be difficult for them to understand what's going on, or worst of all, to no school at all.

We found out that the most badly off were children in remote country areas. In the Highlands of Scotland, for example, the nearest schools for the deaf are hundreds of miles away in Aberdeen and Glasgow.

Building new schools takes time and a vast amount of money, but there could be a solution; a *travelling* school on wheels. A van fitted with all the special equipment that the teacher can actually drive to the children.

John took Blue Peter film cameras to Jersey where a mobile classroom was already in action. Two days with Eric Payne, the driver and teacher, left him in no doubt about its usefulness.

"You wait till you see the film," he said. "There's this little lad called Adam, who is able to keep up with quite difficult arithmetic, thanks to the extra help he's getting. He's seven years old. And Carole, who is thirteen, she's actually able to learn French. She speaks it much better than me—and my hearing's normal!"

I went to Jersey to see a mobile classroom in action. 7-year-old Adam was catching up with his arithmetic.

"It's like a key," said Lesley, after she'd seen the film. "That van's unlocking the door to a whole new life for Adam and . . ."

"That's it!" said Pete. "Key . . . Key-Note. Unlock the door and you hear sounds . . . notes."

"And we could collect keys, too," said Lesley. "If

We reached our Appeal Target by 2 January. It was a marvellous moment when we drove our four Key-Note vans into the studio.

we collected enough, we could buy more of those vans."

"Let's collect cars as well as keys," said John. "I bet there are people who've still got an old dinky or two in their cupboards. And we did very well with old toy cars when we collected them eight years ago. They turned out to be so valuable, we had our very first Blue Peter Auction."

That's how our Key-Note Appeal began. Our target was 2 million parcels and envelopes of old keys and cars. We worked out that they'd provide

four Key-Note vans, and the places where they were needed most badly were Norfolk, Cornwall, the Dyfed area of Wales and the Highlands of Scotland. Altogether, those places had about one thousand five hundred children who'd be able to use those mobile classrooms—if only they had the chance.

Thanks to you, they have!

By 2 January 1978 we'd not only hit the Jackpot—we'd exceeded it! Old keys and cars had come pouring in to our Depot at Lambeth by post, by personal delivery and by Roadline, whose generous offer of free, nationwide delivery meant people could send large and heavy donations without any extra cost. All the collectors' items were set aside to be auctioned. The rest was melted down and sold as scrap metal.

It was a proud moment when we drove our four Key-Note vans into the Blue Peter studio. Not only the vans. Your keys and cars had provided all the special equipment, too.

Expert Mike Martin showed us how the equipment worked and we asked him what we could do with all your extra keys and cars.

Collectors' items like this 1955 Austin A40 weren't melted down. The pedal car was restored to mint condition for our Auction.

"I think video equipment for deaf children in schools is the greatest need, after the vans," said Mike.

A few weeks later he demonstrated how the video kits worked. They included cameras, so that teachers could record lessons to suit individual needs. And with the "freeze frame" device, the tapes could be stopped at any moment when the deaf children couldn't understand what was happening.

These kits could help hundreds of children all over Britain and we hope we'll be able to provide a great many of them.

One of our most unusual donations has been a

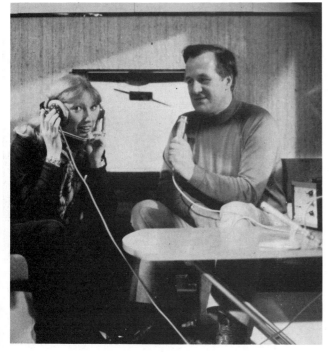

Mike Martin showed us how all the Key-Note van equipment worked.

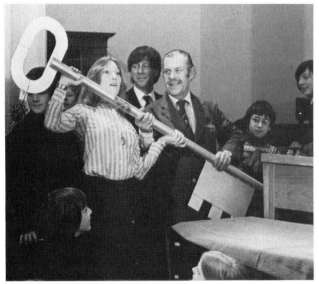

A world record of £370 was paid for this van. In 1934 it cost 4d.

Giant keys like these helped to swell our proceeds. The Auction alone raised £10,597 and 2 pence.

1928 Humber Tourer motor car that was discovered in a barn in Devon rusting away and used as a chicken house. The Royal Agricultural Society gave it to our Appeal and apprentices from the Job Creation Scheme restored it at the Coventry Motor Museum, to be auctioned at the Bank Holiday Town & Country Motoring Festival.

That's the marvellous thing about our Blue Peter Appeals. So many people help in so many different ways. And one thing's certain, it's all the hundreds and thousands of small donations that enable us to reach our Targets. By sending just one key or one toy car, you've helped to unlock the door of the world of sound for thousands of deaf children.

Apprentices working at the Coventry Motor Museum renovated this unusual donation—a 1928 Humber Tourer—a present to the Key-Note Appeal from the Royal Agricultural Society.

MYSTERY PICTURE

① BLACK ⑥ LIGHT GREEN
② YELLOW ⑦ DARK GREY
③ DARK BROWN ⑧ LIGHT BROWN
④ DARK GREEN ⑨ BLUE
⑤ ORANGE ⑩ LIGHT GREY

COLOUR THE SPACES AS INDICATED BY THE NUMBERS AND THE MYSTERY PICTURE WILL APPEAR

37

Map labels:
PORTSMOUTH
RIO/PORTSMOUTH 5,500 MILES
PORTSMOUTH/CAPETOWN 6,650 MILES
RIO DE JANEIRO
CAPE TOWN
AUCKLAND
AUCKLAND/RIO 7,400 MILES
CAPE TOWN/AUCKLAND 7,600 MILES

These were the words on the banner Clare Francis raised high up the mast of her yacht at the end of her round-the-world sail last April. And each time Clare's returned from one of her marathon sails, she's given the impression wild horses wouldn't drive her to do it again!

A year and a half earlier, Clare became the first woman to cross the finishing line in the Single Handed Transatlantic Race.

It had taken her 29 days from leaving Portsmouth—29 days alone on her yacht *Robertson's Golly.* She had sailed through tremendous storms, but even in the worst conditions, she managed to film herself with special cameras given to her by the BBC *World About Us* programme. In one of her last filming sessions as she neared the end of the race she said "Never again . . ."

So when she brought her boat into the Blue Peter studio (the biggest object we've ever had in there) my first question was if she'd changed her mind.

"No," she declared, "never again on my own." But the sea is in her blood. As she said,

"Whenever I'm at sea for a long time, I want to be on land, but as soon as I'm back on land, I'm dying to be back at sea!"

Clare's Round the World yacht *ADC Accutrac.*

The biggest object we've ever had in the studio, Clare's Transatlantic Racing Yacht, *Robertson's Golly*.

It was a filthy day—the wind was howling and rain lashed the deck—not the most pleasant filming assignment. But as I love sailing above almost anything else, I didn't mind. The film director and his unit weren't of the same opinion! Trying to make a film when people are turning green all round you isn't an easy task.

In one of the calmer moments, Clare showed me around the boat that would be her home for several months. It was quite luxurious—there was even a shower, but Clare pointed out that it wouldn't be used much, as it took a lot of their precious fresh water supply. The boat had three toilets—but before the race Clare was having two of them taken out to save weight. All the doors had been thrown away too, to keep the boat as light as possible—all, that is, except one—the toilet door!

Our Blue Peter shelves were dwarfed by Clare's yacht—we couldn't put the mast up, it would have gone through the roof!

Showing me around her boat, she described how she had to live on bananas for a few days as they all ripened together! She'd also taken lots of citrus fruit to keep the scurvy away—as well as tomatoes, eggs, cheese, milk and plenty of tinned food.

And to celebrate her arrival in New York, Clare had kept one bottle of her champagne on one side to drink with her family when they met her.

The Transatlantic Race ended in August 1976 and within weeks Clare was planning a new adventure. This one was to be bigger, more difficult and needed much more planning. She'd decided to enter for the "Whitbread Round the World Race", beginning in August 1977.

She hadn't changed her mind about single-handed racing—for this trip she was taking a crew of 11. Her new boat *ADC Accutrac* was much bigger than *Golly*. It was nearly 20 metres long and 5 metres in the beam! The race was going to be in four stages:
1. Portsmouth—Cape Town
2. Cape Town—Auckland
3. Auckland—Rio de Janeiro
4. Rio de Janeiro—Portsmouth

Altogether, Clare and her crew would be travelling over 27 thousand miles. The whole amazing trip would take around seven months.

But before Clare could even get to the starting line, she had months of work to do.

In June, I went on board *ADC Accutrac* during one of her "work up" sails.

Clare showed me one of the film cameras she took on her single-handed transatlantic voyage.

Clare described the loneliness of the long-distance single-handed sailor.

I joined Clare and her crew on board *ADC Accutrac*.

In the galley, there was a cooker on a gimbal to prevent spillage when the yacht was tossed by the waves. And as feeding twelve people was going to be a mammoth operation there was a large deep freeze as well as a refrigerator.

But the most important piece of equipment was the high powered radio. It was so sensitive that Clare would be able to keep in direct contact with home—even when she was on the other side of the world.

Up on deck, Clare let me take the wheel. Fortunately, I didn't make a complete mess of it—my spare time sailing stood me in good stead.

Clare told me: "Sometimes we'll need two people on the wheel, the power in this boat is phenomenal!"

The race was the experience of a lifetime. While we, in Britain, were shivering at the beginning of winter, Clare was in the hot, steamy tropics. Then she moved on through Antarctica, slipping past gigantic icebergs until she reached Australia (in the middle of a heatwave!).

After Christmas, she set off from New Zealand. And we thought of her in February when she sailed in to Rio de Janeiro—just in time for the Carnival. And we thought she'd be dancing the hours away to the rhythm of the Samba as we'd done, on our Summer Expedition, but from the newspaper reports we read, 50 mm. of rain poured down during the Carnival, drenching everyone!

Clare arrived back in Britain on 26 March exactly 211 days from the time she left. She finished the race in fifth place—a tremendous achievement on her first attempt and one, I'm sure, she'll be proud of for the rest of her life.

I don't know Clare's plans for the future but I bet it won't be long before she sets sail again, despite "Long Time No Sea".

This may look calm, but a Force 9 gale was brewing!

SIMON AND GOLDIE

"Do you like dogs?"
That was just about the first question they asked me when I went to the Blue Peter Office at Television Centre to meet Edward Barnes, Biddy Baxter and John Adcock who's the programme's Assistant Editor. It certainly wasn't what I'd expected!

When I heard that Blue Peter had decided to have a new puppy, and that they hoped I'd be able to look after it, I couldn't have been more delighted. We'd always had dogs on the farm when I was a boy, and I used to help my Dad train his Border Collies. The satisfaction you get from teaching a dog to use its intelligence and obey your commands—because it wants to please you—is enormous.

I first met Goldie when she was five weeks old. All puppies look attractive, but I think a litter of Golden Retrievers takes a lot of beating.

"Golden" really is the right word, and even at five weeks, Goldie and her sister and brothers were starting to show the slightly wavy coat that gives the adult dogs their distinctive feathery look.

Goldie was by far the liveliest of the bunch. She was into everything, the minute your back was turned. And she didn't seem a bit frightened of sudden noises or quick movements. That was a good sign, because a television studio with all its

The seven puppies were Amber's second litter.

unexpected happenings is no place for a nervous dog.

The pups had been weaned, and Goldie had already learned to lap from a saucer, but that didn't stop her trying to get a feed from her mother whenever she had the chance.

Amber's a beautiful 4-year-old Golden Retriever, and if Goldie grows up to look like her Mum, she'll be a knock-out! This was only Amber's second litter, and she probably won't have another. She's an ordinary family pet, not a dog kept for breeding. Like most Golden Retrievers, she has a kind and gentle temperament, and Goldie's sister had already been chosen as a trainee Guide Dog by Blue Peter's friend, Derek Freeman, who's the

Guide Dogs for the Blind Puppy Walking Manager. The pups' father is Angus, one of the dogs specially reared by Derek to sire potential Guide Dogs. Angus is an extremely steady and reliable dog, so the combination of his, and Amber's, characteristics should produce superb pups.

Goldie left the litter and came to live with me when she was seven weeks old. She took to her new life like a duck to water—she didn't bat an eyelid when Shep sniffed around and growled at her, and she seemed to regard the cameras and all the studio equipment as outsize toys left around for her to play with.

I'm enjoying training Goldie very much indeed.

Like Petra, we hope she'll be a dog for all the people who live in places where they aren't allowed to keep animals. And by showing her training on the programme, we hope we're giving some useful hints to all young puppy owners.

A well-trained dog is a pleasure for everyone—I always think it unfair when dogs get blamed just because their owners can't be bothered to look after them properly. So I'm determined to do the best I can for Goldie.

I hope you'll be watching her progress each Monday and Thursday.

Mowgli, Akela, Bagheera—if you're a Cub Scout you'll know at once what these names mean.

But did you know that Lord Baden-Powell who founded the Scouting movement got his ideas from one of Britain's greatest story-tellers—Rudyard Kipling?

For Mowgli, Akela and Bagheera are all characters from Kipling's famous *Jungle Books.*

And if you have read them and enjoyed them, you may be surprised to learn that as well as being a great author, Kipling was also one of Britain's very first motorists, and that is how he came to make his home at Bateman's, a grey stone manor house in Sussex, with the year it was built—1634—carved over the front door.

Kipling and his wife had gone house-hunting in a veteran car called the Locomobile.

As soon as they saw the lovely house, set in the most beautiful gardens, they fell in love with it.

"That's it—that must be our very own house," they exclaimed.

As soon as the sale had been arranged, the owner said curiously, "Now you have really decided, I can ask you something. How are you going to manage getting to and from the station? It's nearly four miles, and I've used up two pairs of horses on the hill here."

Kipling pointed to his motor car. "I'm thinking of using this sort of contraption!"

"Oh, those things haven't come to stay," retorted the owner.

When Kipling met him again, years later, the man confessed that if he had known what Kipling had guessed about the future of the motor car, he would have charged him twice the money!

So Rudyard Kipling settled at Bateman's, and lived there for nearly 35 years. At the the end of his life, he sat down in his study to write his own life story. He called it *Something of Myself* because he was a very

private man who didn't like strangers to intrude. He still kept a lot of himself secret. But today, the books and verses he wrote, and what is left at Bateman's, make Rudyard Kipling come alive.

His parents met at a summer picnic beside Lake

The Locomobile, Rudyard Kipling's treasured car, brought him and his wife to Bateman's.

Rudyard in Staffordshire, which is why they gave their son such a strange name! Immediately they were married, they went to India, where Lockwood Kipling had a job as an art master.

Rudyard Kipling was born in Bombay on 30 December 1865. His childhood was filled with the sounds and colours and scents of India. Devoted Indian servants looked after him, and he was very happy with his parents and little sister.

But the shadow of separation lay over all British families in India, because it was thought no British child could stand up to the climate and diseases. So when Rudyard was six, he was sent "home" to an England he scarcely knew, not to any relations, but to people who fostered children of British parents working overseas.

The little boy was neglected and tormented, and no notice was taken of his rapidly worsening eyesight, so

Rudyard's early childhood was spent in India where his father was a teacher.

But when he was six, he was sent away to England and was very unhappy.

He returned to India as a young man and worked as a journalist.

that he became almost blind. At last, after six years, his mother came home from India, and rescued him from the place he called "The House of Desolation" all his life.

Then things got better; Rudyard was sent to boarding school. He was the only boy in the school who wore glasses, and he was called "Gig-Lamps" or "Giggers" by the other boys, but he was happy there, and made life-long friends.

Years later, when he was a famous author, he wrote a book called *Stalky & Co.* all about the school and the adventures he had with his friends.

When he was 16, his life changed again. His father had got him a job on an Indian newspaper, as a junior reporter, so he went back and rejoined his family.

He was fascinated to be in India again, and his half-forgotten childhood came back clearly. As a journalist, he had to go everywhere, meet everyone, and see all sides of life in British India. During hot, sweaty, sleepless nights he wandered through the streets and bazaars of Indian cities. He soon knew more about India than any other Englishman.

He wrote short stories and verses about all the people he met; at first these were printed in his paper, then they were made up and sold as paperback books on railway bookstalls.

Kipling called these years in India "My seven years hard"—he learned to write during this time, and in India he was quite famous, but he had become sickened and exhausted with the country, and longed to leave. He went back to London, to try to find fame and fortune as a writer.

He found he was already well known for his Indian stories. Before he was 25, Rudyard Kipling's name was known wherever English was spoken or read. Ever since then, he has been famous as a writer about India, although he never went back again, apart from a brief visit two years later.

He married an American lady, Caroline Starr Balestier. They lived in America for some years, then they came back to England and lived in a house near Brighton. They had three children—Josephine, Elsie and John. Kipling was very fond of them all, and particularly of Josephine, the eldest. He loved to play with them, and tell them strange stories about animals—later on, these were published as *Just So Stories*.

1899 was a terrible year for the Kipling family. They had business in America, so they sailed for New York. It was bitter February weather—they had a dreadful crossing, and they were all ill.

Kipling developed pneumonia; he was so seriously ill, Carrie looked after him in a hotel, while journalists from the world's newspapers waited outside for news.

He got better, and on 4 March, he was out of danger, but while headlines proclaimed the good news, there was something he was still too weak to be told.

Josephine was desperately ill with pneumonia as well, and she was too weak to resist it. On 6 March she died, aged six.

Carrie had to attend her daughter's funeral alone. As she hurried back to Kipling's bedside, she realised that if he saw her in mourning he would be alarmed, so she snatched up a red shawl and draped it round her black dress before she went to him.

No one knows how Carrie broke the news to her husband. In *Something of Myself* he says nothing about the loss of the daughter he had loved so much.

They went back to England, with their other children, Elsie and John, but they found the house near Brighton full of memories of Josephine. Kipling's father realised how they felt:

"Rud and Carrie found going back to the Elms much harder and more painful than they had imagined. The house and garden are full of the lost child, and poor Rud told his mother how he saw her when a door opened, when a space was vacant at table, coming out of every green, dark corner of the garden, radiant—and heart-breaking."

So they started house hunting, and that is when they found Bateman's. It was the house of their dreams, and during the next twelve years, while John and Elsie grew up, they were very happy there all together.

They enlarged the beautiful gardens round the house, and Kipling designed a pond in the midst of a rose garden that was a delight to the whole family. In the Visitors' Book, some distinguished visitors had the initials F.I.P. after their names—for Fell In Pond!

There was a river with a watermill in their grounds, so they got a ship's cable, dug a trench and harnessed the mill to make their own electricity.

Kipling was very proud to think he owned a part of England, where people had lived and looked after the land for centuries, and he wrote a book for Elsie and

Bateman's was the house he bought when he became a famous writer.

Kipling was a loving father. He had three children—two girls and a boy.

Elsie, Josephine and John put on plays in the garden for the grown-ups.

On a visit to America, Kipling fell seriously ill.

At the same time, his daughter Josephine caught pneumonia and died.

Although he never got over Josephine's death, Kipling lived to become a great writer.

John called *Puck of Pook's Hill,* where by magic, those people come back to life again—a Roman centurion, a Norman Knight at Arms and old Sussex craftsmen.

On the desk in his study, where he wrote his books, Kipling had a big pewter inkstand, and he scratched on the metal the titles of the books he wrote—many of them still read widely today.

The *Jungle Books* were full tales about Mowgli the Man Cub, who is brought up in the jungle by wise talking beasts, and becomes King of the Jungle when he has learnt the Law that teaches every young animal his position and duties.

"Now this is the Law of the Jungle—as old and as true as the sky:
And the Wolf that shall keep it may prosper, but the Wolf that shall break it must die.
As the creeper that girdles the tree trunk, the Law runneth forward and back,
For the strength of the Pack is the Wolf, and the strength of the Wolf is the Pack."

When Baden-Powell, founder of the Boy Scouts, was begged to start something for younger boys, he turned to the *Jungle Books,* with Kipling's enthusiastic approval. Small boys all over Britain—and soon all over the world—became like Mowgli, and learned the Law from Akela, the Wise Grey Wolf, and Bagheera, the black panther. Together they gave the Grand Howl of the Wolf Cub Pack, and promised to serve their king and country.

All over Britain, men were called on to serve their King and Country in August 1914, when Britain and Germany went to war. The happy life at Bateman's was broken up. John Kipling rushed to enlist in the army. After training, he was sent to France, and six weeks later he was killed at the Battle of Loos. He was eighteen years and six weeks old.

Now Rudyard and Carrie, who had lost their eldest daughter, had now lost their only son. They were sad, not only for themselves, but for the millions of others whose sons and husbands had been killed.

Elsie married, and though her parents were glad of her happiness, Bateman's became an emptier place.

By the end of his life, Kipling saw great changes coming to the British Empire, and to the India he had known so well. He saw the rise of Hitler's Germany and realised that the war in which John had been killed was not the end, but that war would break out between Britain and Germany again.

He was still a national figure, and when he died, in January 1936, he was buried in Westminster Abbey, and you can see a memorial to him there.

He has two other memorials. You can visit Bateman's, which is just as it used to be when he lived there. The study where he wrote his books is unchanged—though perhaps a little tidier now.

But his greatest memorial is his books. Every year they are still bought and read, and every year thousands of children read the *Just So Stories,* and *Stalky and Co.,* and the *Jungle Book* for the first time.

CHRISTMAS GLITTER

These cards are very simple to make, and cheap, too. Apart from the card and glue, you only need a few short pieces of tinsel and scraps of foil. For extra sparkle, finish off the cards with some glitter, if your pocket money allows!

First choose your envelopes. Cut your cards to fit the envelope *when folded in half*. Near the bottom of the card, stick on a tub shape cut from a scrap of coloured foil—a sweet paper or milk bottle top will do.

For the tree itself you'll need three pieces of green tinsel. Put a line of glue up from the centre of the tub nearly to the top—leaving room for the star. Stick on your first piece of tinsel, slightly overlapping the edge of the tub. Glue the other two pieces on either side with the top ends meeting and the bottom ends spread out. Make sure all the strands of tinsel are pointing in a *downwards* direction. Trim off any straggly ends to make the tree a good shape.

Decorations
Cut out a small star from gold or silver foil and glue at the top of the tree. Crumple up small pieces of coloured foil into flattish, round shapes and glue on tree. To trim the edges of the card with glitter, cover the main part of the card with paper, leaving just a narrow edge showing all round. Put clear glue on to this edge, shake glitter over it. Shake the "spare" glitter off on to a bit of newspaper and use again. Put glitter on the star, too.

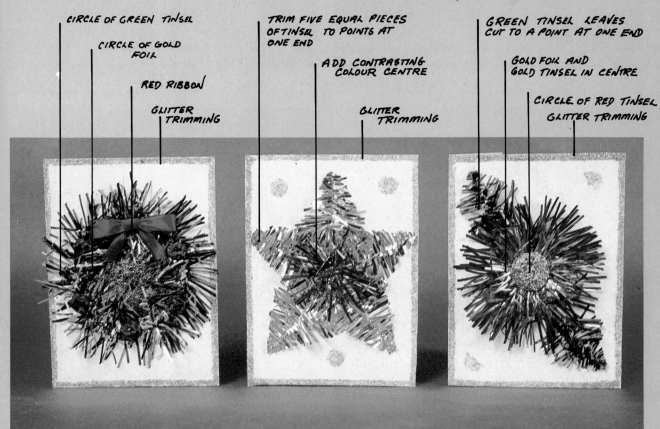

CIRCLE OF GREEN TINSEL
CIRCLE OF GOLD FOIL
RED RIBBON
GLITTER TRIMMING

TRIM FIVE EQUAL PIECES OF TINSEL TO POINTS AT ONE END
ADD CONTRASTING COLOUR CENTRE
GLITTER TRIMMING

GREEN TINSEL LEAVES CUT TO A POINT AT ONE END
GOLD FOIL AND GOLD TINSEL IN CENTRE
CIRCLE OF RED TINSEL
GLITTER TRIMMING

"Unst upon a time", on the northernmost inhabited island in the whole of British Isles, Mrs Hunter had a problem. How to put on the island's production of Dick Whittington. She had the actors and actresses, the costumes, the scenery and a complete stock of theatrical make-up.

The problem? How to use the make-up. No one in the cast, or anyone else on the island for that matter, had a clue how to use the grease paint, and as the island—called Unst by the way—is 50 miles and *two more* islands away from Lerwick, the only sizeable town in the Shetlands, Mrs Hunter was desperate for expert advice.

When she sent her SOS to Blue Peter, we decided the quickest way to help would be to send the vital information via television. Even though most of the people of Unst only get pictures in black and white, it would be more useful and quicker than by post, which often takes ten days to reach the islanders.

With the help of BBC make-up artists Jeni Kine, Sue Bride and Jenny Hughes, we gave an all-purpose, do-it-yourself panto make-up demonstration, as stage by stage we were transformed into an old man, a dame and a cat.

Here's how our transformation took place—and if *you're* putting on a panto this Christmas, we hope you find the tips as useful as the people of Unst did. When Mrs Hunter wrote to say "thank you", she said the Unst Dick Whittington had been a great success and that our panto make-up tips were exactly what they wanted to know.

Like all the best fairy stories, this true tale began with "Unst upon a time . . ." and finished with a very happy ending!

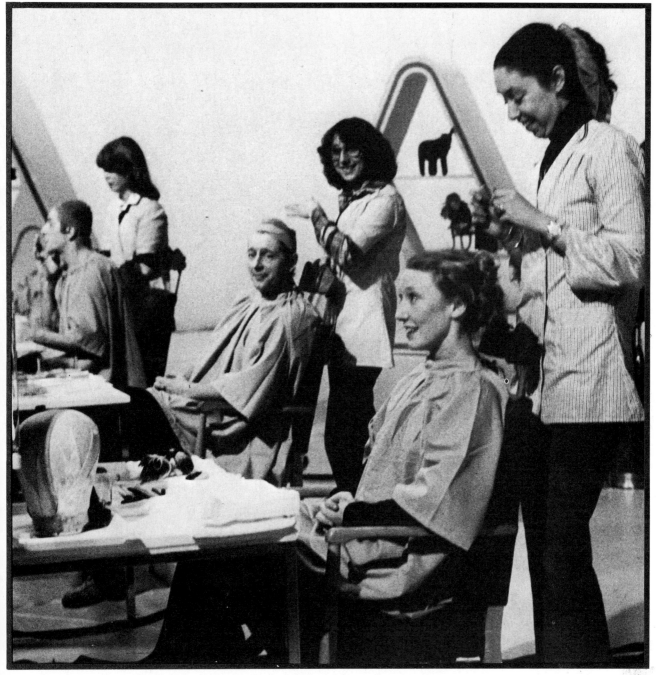

THE OLD MAN

HAIR;
CARPET CANVAS BASE, SOAK IN HOT WATER, CUT FOR EARS AND MOULD TO HEAD

CUT — CUT

SHEEPS WOOL FOR HAIR. KNOT INTO CANVAS WITH LARGE CROCHET HOOK AS IN CARPET KNOTTING.

TRIM HAIR TO YOUR OWN STYLE

MAKE-UP

LEICHNER NO 5 IVORY STICK BASE ALL OVER FACE
NO.16 DARK BROWN SHADING

SHADING

1. AROUND EYES (NOT ON ANY BONES)
2. AROUND FLARE OF NOSTRILS AND UP SIDE OF NOSE
3. BETWEEN NOSE AND LIPS — IN THE MIDDLE
4. BETWEEN LIPS AND CHIN
5. CORNERS OF MOUTH DOWNWARDS
6. LINES ON FOREHEAD
7. SIDE OF EYES ON TEMPLES
8. UNDER CHEEK BONES AND CHIN
9. SMILE LINES NOSE TO MOUTH

HIGHLIGHT ALL SHADING ABOVE AND BELOW WITH NO.5 LEICHNER STICK. POWDER WELL.

NB. GIVE THE OLD MAN BREECHES TUCKED INTO DARK STOCKINGS FOR GAITERS AND A LONG JACKET OVER A WAISTCOAT AND A SHIRT WITH A HIGH COLLAR

A STICK IS ESSENTIAL — IT WILL HELP YOUR AGED WOBBLEY WALK!

PANTOMIME DAME

WIG: CARPET CANVAS BASE, TISSUE PAPER, RAFFIA, SHEEPS WOOL OR CHRISTMAS TREE ANGEL HAIR WIRE COAT HANGER, WALLPAPER PASTE, COLOUR SPRAY.

SOAK CANVAS BASE MOULD TO HEAD ATTACH WIRE FRAME AND COVER WITH TISSUE PAPER.

DECORATE WITH RAFFIA AND SHEEPS WOOL AROUND THE HAIR LINE.

MAKE-UP

LEICHNER NO5 IVORY STICK BASE ALL OVER FACE. MIX WITH CARMINE TO GIVE PINKY TONE.
BRIGHT RED FOR CHEEKS. DARK BROWN FOR FOREHEAD AND SMILE LINES. BLACK FOR THICK EYELINER AND HIGH EYEBROWS (BLOCK OUT REAL EYEBROWS WITH NO.5. WHITE) BRIGHT RED FOR LIPS, THICK EYELASHES GREEN/BLUE EYESHADOW. BREAKFAST CEREAL STUCK ON WITH EYELASH GLUE AND PAINTED DARK BROWN FOR WARTS. POWDER WELL

NB COMPLETE THE EFFECT WITH A LONG BRIGHTLY COLOURED DRESS, APRON, STRIPED STOCKINGS AND SHOES WITH HUGE CARDBOARD BUCKLES.

THE CAT

MASK; CARDBOARD PLASTICINE, BRISTLES FROM OLD BROOM, CORNERS OF POLYSTIRENE MEAT CONTAINER (FOR PUFFY CHEEKS) BLACK BALACLAVA CARDBOARD EARS SEWN ON TOP ELASTIC AROUND MASK

BLACK BALACLAVA WITH CARDBOARD EARS SEWN ON TOP

CUT CORNER FOR RAISED CHEEKS

CARDBOARD   ELASTIC

BRISTLES

PLASTICINE   CORNERS OF POLYSTYRENE MEAT CONTAINER

MAKE-UP

BLACK LEICHNER STICK ALL AROUND MASK ON FACE GREEN LEICHNER STICK FOR EYES WHICH WILL SHOW THROUGH MASK RED LEICHNER FOR LIPS

NB THE CAT MAKE-UP CAN EASILY BE ADAPTED FOR MOUSE. COMPLETE WITH BLACK BODY STOCKING AND BLACK WOOLLY TAIL

Can you solve this case?
Six careless mistakes gave away the crook.
We spotted them—can you?

THE CASE OF THE CUP THAT CHEERS

Bob McCann lifted the F.A. Cup in triumph above his head.

"I've always wanted to do that," grinned Bob, a midfield player for a small-time soccer side called Rosgill Town. He looked sheepishly at his uncle, Detective Inspector McCann.

"Well, this is the only chance you'll get. You haven't got much chance of beating Bidchester United," smiled McCann.

For little Rosgill Town, it was the match of a lifetime—the non-league club was drawn against the cup holders, mighty Bidchester United of Leicester in the third round of the F.A. Cup.

And the Football Association had given permission for the incomparable trophy to be put on display at Rosgill's tiny ground—a tribute to the gallant cupfighting exploits of the south coast soccer minnows.

"I'd better take it," said club director Stan Tipping, and carried the greatest trophy in English football to the safety of the board-room.

"It's good of you to come and keep an eye on the cup," said Bob. "It'll be a great thrill for the Rosgill fans to see it, and we'd never have been allowed to show it here if you hadn't agreed to come and keep guard."

"How do you think you'll get on this afternoon?" queried McCann. "I should think Bidchester are feeling pretty confident just now."

"Well, their star striker Bert Humphrey can't play. He got a bad head injury against an Italian club last week, and he's still in hospital over there. That means they won't be at full strength. So the rest of the team won't be lying in their beds taking it easy this morning."

"How do you know?" asked McCann.

"I spoke to their manager at their hotel first thing. He was taking his lads over to the athletics ground to practise set pieces as soon as they had finished breakfast."

"Are you nervous?" quizzed McCann.

"A little bit," admitted Bob, and looked around the empty terraces that were soon to be packed out by Bidchester's chanting, cheering Blue Army.

But now, the only people stirring were BBC technicians setting up their cameras for *Match of the Day*. . . and a busy-looking track-suited little man coming out of the stands with a bulging kit bag.

"Hoots, mon, it's a grand day for it," he called as he walked over to Bob and the grey-suited figure of the policeman.

"Can't wait to get out on the park," said Bob amiably. "I'm Ally McMilne," grinned the little man, proferring his hand. "I'm Bidchester's physiotherapist."

"We're glad to meet you," said Bob. "I'm playing left midfield for Rosgill, and this is my uncle,

Detective Inspector McCann."

"Is that so?" asked McMilne, with a wary look in his eye.

"Don't worry," smiled Bob. "He's only here to watch over the F.A. Cup. But how's Humphrey? I read about his injury this morning."

"Och, the wee laddie's fine just now. I bandaged up his foot before the coach left Bidchester this morning."

"It must seem strange coming down to play in a little place like this," said Bob, modestly, looking around the weed-grown terracing and ramshackle stands on the compact Rosgill ground.

"Well, that's football, son," said McMilne. "One match you're playing a cup final at White City Stadium . . . and just a few short months later you're fighting for your lives in a funny old place like this. It's the variety of life that makes a career in football so great."

"I suppose you get used to all this television, but it makes me jolly nervous," said Bob as he watched the BBC men mounting a camera on the roof of the stand.

"Aye—I ken Dickie Davies and the rest of the boys from *Match of the Day* very well. They're a great set o' lads, and they know their football."

"What's your worst moment as a physio?" asked Bob, hoping to learn a little about the secret life of the greatest footballing club in the land.

"That was when our young coloured boy, Lukie Mather, broke his leg in two places in a semi-final. But would you believe it? The plucky wee fella got up and carried on. Can you imagine it? Playing forty minutes wi' a broken leg! That's what I call a footballer."

"Gosh," said Bob, looking up at the menacing clouds that appeared, rolling towards them from the English Channel. "I hope the weather holds good," he added. "This is one match I don't want to have to play in the pouring rain."

"I shouldna bet your boots on it," said McMilne. "There was three feet of snow on the ground this morning as the lads were driving through East Anglia."

A hoarse cry interrupted their conversation.

"McCann! McCann!" The portly figure of director Tipping came racing across the pitch. "The Cup, the Cup!" he cried. "They've stolen the Cup."

"Settle down now," said McCann, calmly silencing the panting, ashen-faced official. "Tell me precisely what has happened."

"I left the cup in the board-room—then I went over to check the visitor's dressing-room. I went back and it was gone." Tipping buried his face in his hands. "I'll never be able to hold up my head again. I've just lost the most important trophy in the history of the game," he sobbed.

"Well, I'll be away to prepare my embrocation," said McMilne, picking up the massive kit bag.

"I don't think that will be necessary," said McCann drily. "Even if you had the knowledge to do it."

"What do you mean?" blustered McMilne. "I haven't time to bother with the likes of you the noo," he said, vaulted the barrier and made for the gate.

"Stop him, Bob!" rasped McCann, and Rosgill's plucky midfielder sprinted after the Scotsman, and with a magnificent flying tackle, he pulled the legs from under the fleeing physio.

It was the most important professional foul of his career.

McMilne made a grab for the kit bag, but the detective was there first. "I'll have that," he said, coolly.

"What are you doing to our guest?" expostulated Tipping.

For answer, McCann unzipped the physio's bag and revealed the F.A. Cup in all its gleaming glory.

"Does this answer your question?" queried McCann to the aghast figure of the director.

"How—how did you know?" asked Tipping.

"He made six very foolish mistakes. Bob's foul tackle has put an end to the phoney physio's football career—three hours before the match has even started."

Did you spot the six mistakes?
Check your answers on page 76.

The secret life of

LUCY MATHEN

she'd been playing classical guitar.

"Only about a week," she said. "My real instrument is *bass* guitar."

Before I had time to look surprised—not many women even try to handle a big, powerful bass—she dropped her next bombshell.

"You see, I play in a rock band. Hey, why don't you come and hear us one evening?"

This made me so curious I asked her if she'd extend the invitation and let me take the Blue Peter cameras to follow a whole day in the life of Lucy Mathen.

"OK," she said.

We always look forward to the ALL STAR RECORD BREAKERS. It's the only time in the year when all the people who appear in Children's Programmes can get together for one show. We like it, partly because we get a chance for a gossip with people who work on other shows, but mainly because we all have to do something different.

I go back to dancing for a day, Johnny goes back to acting, and I think everyone was surprised to find that Pete has such a strong singing voice.

But the person who caught everybody's eye last Christmas was Lucy Mathen. We were all used to seeing her bobbing up all over the country doing reports for John Craven's *Newsround*, but frankly, we all wondered what she was going to do in a musical show.

We found out when the Producer gave us all guitars and told us we were going to accompany Lucy and Keith Chegwin whilst they played a guitar duet.

During a break in rehearsals, I asked Lucy how long

9.00. And fifteen of the most hectic hours of my life begin when I meet Lucy and her crew outside the Mosque School in Hounslow. It's a Lucy Mathen News Report: Moslems are campaigning for the government to allow them to run their own religious schools. The Mosque School Lucy is reporting looks just like an ordinary suburban house from the outside. She leads me and the crew inside (we all have to take off our shoes) and work begins.

9.10. "Get some shots of the teachers asking questions, and some nice big close-ups of the children answering," Lucy tells Eddie Smales, her News cameraman. "Then we'll do an interview outside and finish up with my piece to camera."

"Lovely," says Eddie. "Right—camera here. And a couple of broads at the back should light it."

Lucy peers down the viewfinder of the camera:
"That's fine," she says.

9.30. We move outside and Lucy starts her interview with Dr Posha, the man behind the campaign. I help by keeping the children quiet during the filming, while Lucy gets her story.

10.00. Interview over. The crew sets up to shoot Lucy's introduction, which, when the film is put together, is the first thing the viewers will see. Eddie wants Lucy to stand on a box so that he can get the Mosque School sign in the shot behind her.

"But I'll look about 3 metres tall," protests Lucy.

"I promise you nobody will know you're standing on a box," says Eddie.

But Lucy isn't happy, and in the end they lower the camera and she stands on the floor.

11.00. Blue Peter filming can last all day—and even longer! But for a news reporter, it's all different. Two hours at top speed, and already filming is complete and the crew are packing up their gear. A despatch rider arrives to collect the film and roars off to the Television Centre. He has to catch the bath in the processing laboratories, or the film will not be developed in time for the bulletin. Lucy and I pile into her tiny Fiat 500 and make for the *Newsround* office. She has a script to write in a hurry. . . .

12.00. John Craven is on the phone to New York. He waves to Lucy and mouths: "Was it cold?"

"Freezing!" Lucy mouths back.

"How long do you think it's going to be?" asks Jill Roach, the *Newsround* Editor.

"Dr Posha was quite good—and the children looked very nice—about 1 minute 30 seconds."

Jill mutters some figures to herself and looks down at the running order of the bulletin.

"That might mean dropping the Newcastle story—so your piece had better be good."

A loudspeaker on the wall crackles.

"Service Desk," says a voice. "Reports are coming in of an explosion in a chemistry lab. in a south London school."

Everybody freezes. Jill looks up.

"Right—that's the lead if we can get a crew there. Newcastle's definitely out. And Lucy—one thirty and no more—O.K.?"

"O.K.," shouts Lucy, and we disappear to the cutting room.

12.30. The film is rushed up from the laboratories: Nick, the film editor, and Lucy look at everything that was shot that morning—just a few hours ago—and decide what to keep, and what to throw away.

"You've got to be ruthless," explains Lucy, "and just keep the stuff that tells the story. O.K., Nick, it's my intro—G.V. (general view) Mosque School, 10 secs. Close up teacher, 5 secs. Children, 5 secs. And interview as we discussed. Absolute max. 1.30 Jill said." Lucy grabs my hand and we dash back to the office to write the commentary, picking up a sandwich and a cup of coffee on the way.

4.00. The temperature is rising in the Newsroom. Nobody speaks now—except to mutter at their typewriters. Deadline looms ever closer.

"An experiment goes wrong in a school laboratory," whispers John to himself. "Fifteen people are hurt."

"At the moment, Britain's 200,000 Moslem population . . ." types Lucy, mouthing the words.

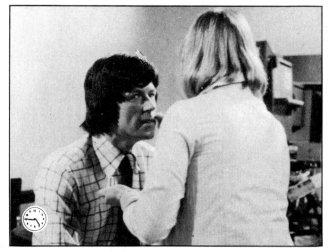

4.45. The *Newsround* Studio. John is having his face powdered at the same time as he checks the script with the Studio Director.

The Director's voice booms out:

"Pages 1 and 2, School Lab. explosion. Cut to film on TK 31. Pages 3 & 4 John intros Moslem school. Cut to film TK 32. Second voice Lucy."

Lucy bursts into the studio . . . script completed with just fifteen minutes to spare.

"Where do I sit?" she asks John.

"Over here by me."

5.00. "Stand by TK 31 & 32. Stand by Studio!" says the Studio Director. "10, 9, 8, 7, 6. . . ."

It seems just a few minutes ago since we were standing outside that freezing Mosque School—and now, miraculously, the report was going out on the air with all the calmness of a routine operation.

"At the moment, Britain's thousands of Moslem children go to ordinary schools. . . ."

5.06. Suddenly, it's all over. There's a quick meeting about what *might* be in the bulletin tomorrow and Lucy and I dash for the car park and whirl back to her flat. There's another deadline to meet now.

6.00. Over a quick meal of baked beans, Lucy tells me about her other life.

"We have this rock band. We only started six months ago. We're called *Startled Saint,* after the pub where we played our first gig." (A gig, I discovered, is a one-night stand.)

"Why a pub?" I asked her.

"Pubs are the only places you can get when you're starting off," Lucy explains. "It can be quite tough, because the customers don't always like rock music—or us! We have to try and win them over. It's a pretty tricky pub we play tonight."

"Who else is in the band?"

"There's Nuala, the lead singer—she's a teacher; her husband, Andy, on drums; Ray, who works for Lifeboats, plays guitar and sings; Mark, a computer technologist, on lead guitar—he can be brilliant; and me, on bass."

"How did you all get together?" I asked.

"Well, Ray, Mark and I have been friends since university, and then another friend introduced us to Nuala and Andy—and we discovered we were five people in search of a rock band.

6.30. The rest of the band arrive and we start loading up the van with all the gear—it seems a massive load for five musicians.

"We're only driving you about 200 yards," bellows Mark, "but we need a big van because we've got so much equipment—we go for a big sound!"

7.00. We start setting up the mikes, amplifiers and speaker cabinets—everything must be in the right place or the sound the band aim for is destroyed. A couple of Lucy's friends arrive and give a hand. Mark looks for the power source, the electricity for three strident guitars and two gutsy voices, while Ray helps Andy with the big, resonant drums. But Andy won't let anyone touch his delicate cymbals.

"Once we blew all the lights in a pub," says Ray. "We had to play without mikes."

"What was it like?" I ask.

"Terrible!" he laughs.

Deep, bell-like sounds are booming out over the pub as Lucy begins to tune up, standing in front of her huge speaker cabinet—as tall as she is, and much noisier.

8.00. "OK then—everyone ready?" asks Ray.

The tuning up stops. Everybody nods. Conversation in the pub dies down, and I go to take a seat in the audience.

"Right—we'll start with Lucy's number. A-one, two, three, four. . . ." His heel bangs out the rhythm on the stage and the band takes off. . . playing a number called "Electric Bass" written especially for Lucy.

Lucy's fingers fly over the heavy-gauge strings as she plays the intricate bass patterns . . . a good bass sound is the heart of a rock band.

Ray and Nuala approach the microphones to sing: "She's not just a pretty face, she just wants to Pl..a..a..ay.. Electric Bass! Electric Bass!"

9.30. After 4 more numbers from the band, Ray surprises the audience and amazes me by suddenly announcing: "Ladies and gentlemen, Lesley Judd of Blue Peter is going to join us in the next number. . . ."

11.00. The band rock into their final number as last orders are served. The audience shouts for more, but time has run out. Humping time again: and we load up the van to go home.

12.00. "It went quite well tonight, I thought," said Ray.

"Not bad," said Lucy.

"Tomorrow night we're at the Tulse Hill Tavern."

"Oh, goody," said Lucy.

"And what about tomorrow morning?" I asked as we climbed into the van.

"I'm doing a story at London Zoo at 9 o'clock," she yawned: it had been quite a day.

Goodbye Petra

Thursday, 23 March 1978 was a momentous day for me. It was the day that the large bronze statue of Petra was erected by the front gates at Television Centre—and it was my last day as a regular member of the Blue Peter team.

It was the end of a chapter in the history of Blue Peter, and for John and Lesley and me, it was an extremely moving moment when we saw William Timym's superb sculpture finally in position by our Tree for the Year Two Thousand.

The suggestion for the sculpture came from Blue Peter viewers all over Britain. When Petra died, we had thousands of letters. About half of them contained donations in remembrance of Petra to be put towards some good cause, or to go towards an animal charity of our choice. The others asked if it would be possible to have a statue erected in Petra's honour. And Tim suggested he sculpted a large, bronze head of her, that could be put up out-of-doors at Television Centre for everyone to see.

We all liked the idea of a canine "blue plaque". The houses of many well-known people are identified in this way—so why shouldn't a famous TV star be given the same kind of honour?

Petra had undoubtedly made history. She'd clocked up an amazing one thousand one hundred and ninety-two appearances on the programme. And as she'd come and gone through the Main Gates of the BBC's Television Centre every week for almost the whole of her life, we could think of no better place for Tim's bronze than just inside those gates, next to our Blue Peter silver birch and the box we buried for the Year Two Thousand—which includes her photograph, as well as those of Jason and Patch.

One day last October, we took our cameras outside and watched Tim decide exactly where he wanted his sculpture to stand. He made some lightning sketches, too.

"For out-of-doors, it's best for the head to be a little larger than life size," he explained.

"Like your bronze lion's head at London Zoo?" we asked.

"Exactly," said Tim. "And we'll need a plinth to raise it up."

The plinth was a problem. Stone would have been ideal, but it was far too expensive. There was no alternative but concrete—or so we thought at the time.

But while Blue Peter was actually "on the air", the telephone lines to our office were buzzing.

"I've just seen your programme—I'd like to give

you some granite for your plinth."

"Would you like some granite from the original London Bridge that was shipped to America?"

Altogether we had dozens of offers of help, and in the end, to be fair, we decided to accept the very first suggestion.

It came from David Ridgeway, the owner of a quarry at Gelli in South Wales. Very appropriately, his stone was called Blue Pennant, and it was a hard sandstone so tough and durable it was actually being used to repair the Tower of London!

Tim was delighted.

"It couldn't be more perfect for my bronze," he said. "It's the best stroke of luck we could have possibly had!"

I knew from years back, when Tim had sculpted the small bronze of Petra that we keep on our studio shelves, that the head wouldn't happen overnight. Sculpting is a long and complicated business and it starts with making the figure in modelling clay. Last time, though, Tim had Petra herself to model from. When I took Blue Peter film cameras to his studio in Hampstead, I wondered how on earth Tim was going to tackle his larger than life size head.

I found him surrounded by drawings—all the ones he'd made of Petra in 1977 and a load of tangled wire. But when I looked closely, the wire was knotted and twisted into a very definite dog shape.

"This is the armature," explained Tim. "It's made from wood and wire—it has to be pretty strong, because I have to cover it with plasticine."

"What did you make this from? Enlarged drawings?" I asked.

"Yes," replied Tim. "And you can see how the armature fits into these dimensions, so I know I'm making it exactly to the right scale. The next thing is to cover it with plasticine."

I watched, fascinated, as Tim deftly moulded lengths of the modelling clay over the wire.

"We establish the bone structure first of all. You see where the eye socket comes about here—leave the eye to the last because that is the most important part—to give the expression of the dog. We leave that till the end. First I want to get the complete outline of Petra, and then when this is done, you get the bone structure perfectly correct, then I start the details."

Three weeks later, Blue Peter cameras and I paid another visit to Tim. This time we went to the Sculpture Casting Studio near High Wycombe, where the actual casting of the bronze was to be made.

It was easy to tell why sculpting in bronze is a lengthy business. Tim had decided to use something called the "lost wax" process, which meant making a plaster cast of his model head and pouring liquid rubber into the plaster to make a mould.

The rubber was left to form a skin between the modelling clay and the plaster. When the outer case was taken off, Petra's profile was already clear. But the important surface was *inside* the rubber. The mould was going to have to work

Tim began modelling Petra's head by making an armature from wood and wire.

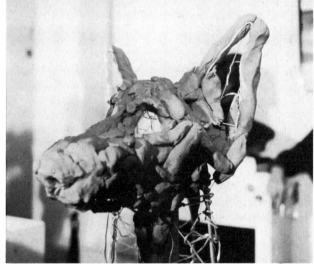

As he covered it with modelling clay, a definite dog-shape emerged.

At the foundry, a plaster cast of the head was made and liquid rubber poured inside to form a mould.

rather like a photographic negative; a perfect copy of the original in reverse, so that it could reproduce every detail of Tim's modelling onto another material. And that material was wax. The whole aim at the end of *fifteen* processes, was to produce a rigid ceramic mould of Tim's sculpture for molten bronze to be poured into. To do this, a wax replica had to be made that could later be melted out of the ceramic. Hence the name, the "lost wax" process.

The whole process took five days and it was an

agonising moment when the plaster casing was split away. If anything had gone wrong, Tim would have to start all over again. But the wax replica was perfect. All Tim had to do was to retouch a few small details—it was the last time Petra's head would be soft enough to make any alterations. And as a finishing touch, Tim signed his name in the wax.

Last of all came the most dramatic moment: the casting of the molten bronze. The ceramic mould had been fired in a kiln overnight to make it extra hard, and for four hours the bronze had been heated in a furnace to reach the colossal temperature of 1250 degrees centigrade.

Only fifteen minutes later the bronze had cooled sufficiently for the sand, which was packed around the mould, to be knocked away. It had taken over two weeks to produce the bronze cast and only when most of the ceramic had been cleaned off could we tell if the cast was a good one.

It was perfect!

"It's absolutely marvellous—a superb cast," said Tim. "But it's not quite finished," he told me. "We must get the markings of Petra. You see, the spots over the eyes, they are light, and then this side here, a light part. A black nose, a bit of light around the nose. A little bit in the ears, a light in the ears. It's very important."

Tim is a perfectionist. By the time he'd finished, there was no way in which Petra's bronze head could be improved.

But before it could be erected, the plinth it was to stand on had to be quarried. So Blue Peter cameras and I set off for Wales.

With the Brecon Beacons, Pontypridd and the start of the Rhondda Valley in the background, the views from the quarry at Gelli were fabulous. David Ridgeway was there to meet us and he took me on a guided tour.

"The quarry's in two parts," he explained. "There's the masonry part—with stones for walls, crazy paving and monumental work, and the area where the stones that are unsuitable for masonry are crushed and processed for road stones. Most of Britain's motorways are made from Blue Pennant stone."

I reckoned if Blue Pennant was tough enough for the M1, it would be able to stand up to the wear and tear of the south-west London winds and rain.

David took me to see some newly-blasted stone so that he could choose a suitable block for the plinth.

"When you start doing something as important as a plinth, how do you choose the rock?" I asked.

"You have to find a piece larger than the size you want," said David, and pointed to a massive piece of stone which he marked with an X for identification.

David explained that the job of cutting and inscribing such hard stone is one for a highly skilled craftsman. His most experienced mason, Des Wilkins, was to work on Petra's plinth.

"It's a pretty big stone. Where do you start?" I asked Des.

The next stage was the making of a wax replica, and Tim signed his name at the bottom.

Foundry manager, Ted Knell, added Petra's markings with the aid of acid and a blow torch.

The quarry at Gelli in South Wales gave us the Blue Pennant Stone for the plinth.

"First of all, I'll measure it up," he replied. "The only thing is, there's a little shake there."

"A what?" I asked

"A shake," said Des.

"A shake?"

"Like a flaw, yes." And the first thing Des did was to chip off the offending shake. He used equipment that have been the tools of the trade for masons for

I used a "pitcher" to help chip the massive block of stone into shape.

how difficult it was!

Once the plinth had been cut to size, it took Des almost a week to carve the inscription. We'd decided on something quite simple—just

PETRA
1962-1977

with our Blue Peter ship underneath. When I returned, the plinth looked beautiful. Its rugged shape had kept all the natural lines of the sandstone, and would set off the bronze much better than smooth concrete would have done.

One blustery day in the middle of March, the thousand kilo plinth travelled by lorry from Wales to London, and I was there with a massive tower crane to watch it being winched into place.

Tim and David supervised the operation and made sure it was exactly in line with the silver birch trees—just as Tim had described it when he made his very first sketches.

A few days later, on 23 March, on my last Blue Peter, we took our studio cameras outside for the actual erection of the bronze head.

Lesley poured liquid concrete onto the top of the plinth, and John and I carried the head from the foundry van and lifted it on to the plinth.

Tim was there to guide us, and when we all stood back to see Petra's head in its full glory, it was one of my most moving moments on the programme.

I had quite a lump in my throat as we thanked Tim. Dear old Petra—she truly was "a dog for everyone". Now—thanks to Tim's bronze, she'll be remembered by all the visitors to the studios where she worked for almost 15 years.

hundreds of years. A great contrast with the modern machinery in the rest of the quarry. And working by hand it took a couple of days to cut the block of stone down to the size Tim had specified.

Des very trustingly let me have a go, and armed with a "pitcher" (a chisel-like tool with an extremely sharp blade) I actually chipped a piece of the Blue Pennant into shape. Des had made it look so easy, it wasn't until I took over that I realised just

No need to introduce Bjorn, Anni-Frid, Agnetha and Benny or Showaddywaddy who've all appeared on Blue Peter during the past year. But do you recognise *this* pop star?

He's the 15-year-old schoolboy who rose to fame when he was picked to play the part of the Young Elvis Presley in the spectacular Elvis musical.

From a sixth-former at school in Bury St Edmunds to a leading part in a West End theatre must be a record-breaker. Tim Whitnall had had no previous stage experience, but he'd always been an Elvis fan—and a Blue Peter fan, too. He won his

V.I.P.S.
Very Important POP STARS

first badge when he was eleven, and when he joined us on the programme last November, we awarded Tim a silver badge for his outstanding achievement.

SEEING STARS

Astronomers claim that there are 100,000,000,000 visible stars in our galaxy. The nearest one is about 25 million miles away.

If you're like me, you'll probably be able to spot the North Star and, perhaps, the Great Bear, but that's about all. Mind you, since I got my Christmas present, a star gazing umbrella, Purves has become a budding Patrick Moore. All I have to do is point the brolly at the North Star and twist it until the stars marked on the plastic match those in the sky. Then I just read off the names, like Andromeda, Cygnus and Ursa Minor. It's a clever invention and one I thought was brand new—but I was wrong. It turned out to be a 68-year-old idea!

The day after I showed the brolly on the programme, a letter arrived in the Blue Peter office from a Mrs Williamson of Helensburgh in Scotland. She wrote:

"The original Starry Umbrella was patented by my father around the year 1910 to accompany a book published at the same time to teach astronomy."

Nothing's new! The book was called *Guide to the Starry Heavens* by Duncan McEwan. And Mrs Williamson also sent us a photograph of her father with his umbrella. It looked just like mine, except that the stars were printed on black silk—plastic hadn't been invented then!

The original "starry umbrella" was invented by the Scottish astronomer Duncan McEwan 68 years ago.

63

Star maps and guides have been around for centuries. We showed one in the studio that we borrowed from the Royal Astronomical Society. It was called "*Urania's Mirror or A View from the Heavens*", and at one hundred and fifty years old, it was a rare collector's item. It was a box full of hand-coloured cards that showed the main groups of stars like Leo Major and Minor, and Scorpio. The backs of the cards were covered in tissue paper, and holes had been punched through the card wherever there was a star. Holding them up to the light, the patterns of stars were clearly visible. You can try this for yourself if you take a safety pin and carefully prick the stars in the pictures below.

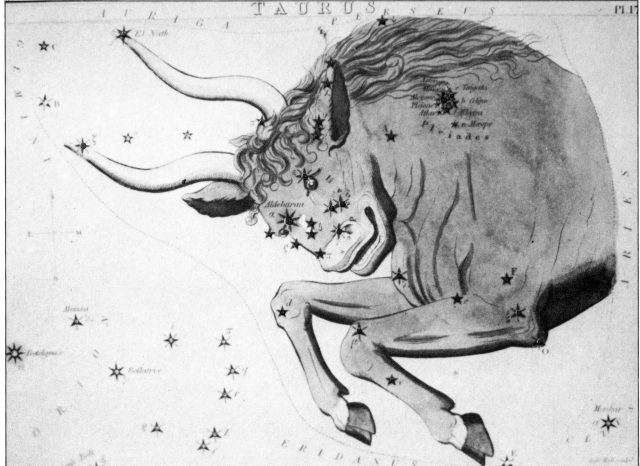

When you hold the page up to a light, you'll see the patterns of Taurus.

If you want to take a first step in astronomy, here's a start. Below is a picture of the night sky as it will be in January 1979. Hope it's not cloudy!

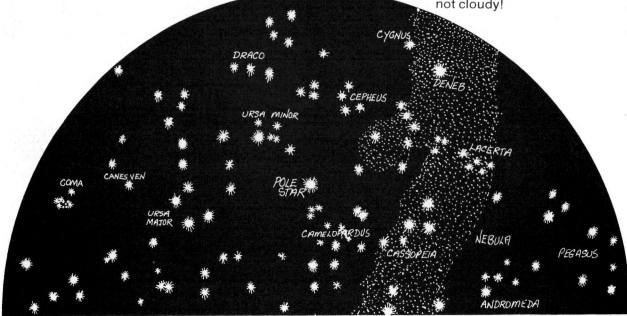

PETE GOES TO KNIGHT SCHOOL

I've always secretly fancied myself as a knight. *Sir* Peter Purves has a certain ring to it—don't you think? It's never been easy to become a knight. Today, knighthoods are given for services to the Queen, which really means being a thumping success at almost anything—a jockey, like Sir Gordon Richards—a poet, like Sir John Betjeman—or even running holiday camps like Sir Billy Butlin.

Since television began in 1936 there have only been four knighthoods given for "services to television"—and they were all for the bosses, so my chances of becoming a 20th-century knight didn't seem too great. But, I thought, in days of old when knighthoods were given for valour, honour and chivalry, it would have been a different story—or would it?

Pedro—the Idle Charger.

I discovered that you weren't just *made* a knight in the olden days—you had to train, and the training began at the age of eight. You started as a page which meant becoming a general dogsbody in a knight's household whilst you learnt the knightly skills of jousting and quintaining as well as playing the mandolin, speaking Latin and learning how to behave chivalrously to ladies. At fourteen, if you had made the grade, you would become a squire which was a knight's special attender, whilst your training continued until you were eighteen. Then, provided you were well born, owned land and were accomplished at all the knightly arts, and swore undying loyalty to the sovereign, you would achieve the status of knighthood.

Even if it was still 12th century, I thought, I'd left it all a bit late. It was then I saw the advertisement:

*Knight's Training Course. Learn to be
a knight at the British Jousting Centre.
Full elementary weekend course
available to males and females aged
14–50. Apply to the Principal, British
Jousting Centre, Chilham Castle, Kent.*

My plumes are black for the Black Gauntlet—yours are blue for Blue Peter and red for blood!

I attack—you parry!

So the next weekend I drove down to Chilham Castle where I met Max Diamond, alias the Knight of the Black Gauntlet. When I arrived he was wielding a huge two-handled sword in combat with two other "trainee" knights. He took off his "helm" which entirely covered his head to reveal a face like Don Quixote, complete with curly white hair and flowing moustache. I asked him what gave him the idea of a School for Knights.

"Well, Peter," he said, leaning forward on the hilt of his sword. "I think that a lot of people would like to bring back—even for a few hours—some of the splendour and chivalry and pageantry of those olden days."

To take part in some of that splendour, Max helped me into the gear for a fight with broad swords.

"I prefer the helm to a visor, Peter," he said, encasing my face in a huge, inverted coal scuttle, "because if a lance hits a visor, it would knock the visor up and smash your face in—which is dangerous."

I agreed with the idea that smashing my face was a bit on the dangerous side.

"Now we've got plumes on top of the helm, Peter, because once you've got it on, you've lost your identity."

"I've got black plumes for the Black Gauntlet," he boomed from inside the helm, "and you've got blue and red. Blue's for Blue Peter—and red's for blood! Right, I'll call the shot—and you try to parry—Go!"

The broad sword was so heavy it took most of my strength to lift it off the ground—let alone parry the great, murderous swings of the Black Gauntlet.

"Cheek"—clang!
"Head"—clang!
"Flank"—clang!
"Head"—thud!

I was completely off balance for the last swing—so I thrust my shield into the air and hoped for the best.

"That was good, Peter! Fabulous! Right, let's have a go at the quintaining."

Quintaining is a mounted sport. The knight has to

charge with a lance at a wooden figure of a warrior called a quintain which is mounted on a pivot. The snag is that the quintain has a chain with a spiked ball in his right hand which swings round when you hit him with the lance, and if you're not travelling fast enough, you get the return blow in the back of your neck.

When I told Max that I didn't want a particularly spirited horse, he grinned and said:

"That's all right, Peter, Pedro won't run away with you!"

After the initial walk through to get my bearings, I went back to the start mark, tucked my lance firmly under my arm, gritted my teeth and shouted:

"Come on, Pedro!"

I dug in my heels and prepared to thunder down the field.

Pedro began to amble—and after a lot of encouragement—not to say threats—he broke into something between a walk and a trot.

I struck the quintain on the shoulder with my lance, and as Pedro strolled through, I got the spiked ball right between the shoulders.

"Oh, you *naughty* Pedro!" called Max.

That was my training.

In the afternoon I was to take part in a medieval joust. The British Jousting Association turned out in full costume—and for a few hours we travelled—tardis-like—back into the 12th century.

The tournament began with the knights assembled on horseback in a long line.

"Knights, show your respect," called the Knight of Black Gauntlet.

To a fanfare of trumpets we dipped our lances in allegiance to the Sovereign. Chivalry was the hallmark of the ancient knights. Your opponent was fought fearlessly, but strictly within the Rules of Combat. An unchivalrous action—or an un-knightly deed—was foul play and was not to be tolerated. Knights were often the champions of "fair ladies" and carried their favours into combat.

We were divided into two houses for our tournament. I was in the Blue House, and I carried Lesley's scarf in my belt for a favour.

Pedro was decked out as Knight's Charger, and the costume seemed to inspire him. I wouldn't go so far as to say that he *charged* at the quintain, but he moved *just* fast enough for me to avoid another embarrassing clout on the back of the neck.

Jousting is the most famous and the most dangerous of all the knightly combats. The knights ride full speed towards each other on either side of a fence which is called a "tilt". Armed with a 4-metre lance, they meet at an impact speed of 80 mph. It was because so many deaths were caused by jousting in the 10th and 11th centuries that the first Rules of Combat were drawn up.

I was drawn in the lists to meet the Black Gauntlet myself. I only had time to practise this at walking pace, so I felt a bit fluttery under my chain-mail when the trumpeter sounded the order to charge. Max had promised not to take any unnecessary risks, but I needn't have worried, Pedro wasn't taking any risks at all! He kept so far away from the tilt that I couldn't even *see* Max, let alone hit him!

I began to get the feeling that, unlikely as it seems, I stood a slightly better chance of being knighted for services to television than I would have done as a knight of old.

But Max would have none of it.

"Considering you only started this morning, and you've never done it before in your life—I think you're fabulous."

"Well, that's very kind . . ." I began.

"Kneel down, my boy," he commanded.

I knelt obediently at his feet whilst he tipped me on the shoulder with his great, two-handed sword.

"Arise, Sir Peter," he boomed, "Knight of the Sore Saddle."

Pedro and I stroll into battle.

Knights of Blue Peter

Have a jousting tournament in your own sitting room!

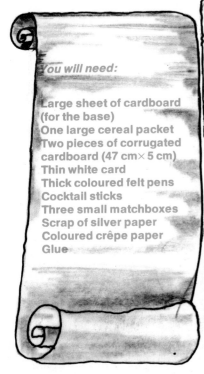

TENTS

1 Cut a piece of card 22 cm × 10 cm and mark stripes along it with a felt tip pen.
Glue the short ends together and opposite the join, cut a slit for the door to within 1 cm of the top.

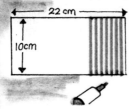

Bend over one side to make the tent flap.

2 For the roof, cut a circle of card approximately 15 cm diameter, mark a cross with a felt tip pen, make a second cross between this one and continue until the circle is covered. Then mark a thick band with felt tip all around the edge.

Cut slits 1.5 cm deep and about every 1 cm round the outside edge, then round off each little flap to make the edging.

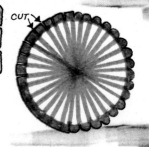

CUT

Cut out a quarter of the circle *and* the first little flaps on one side, make a small hole in the centre and draw into a cone shape by overlapping the cut edge, then glue down. When firmly set, glue the roof onto the rest of the tent.

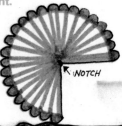

NOTCH

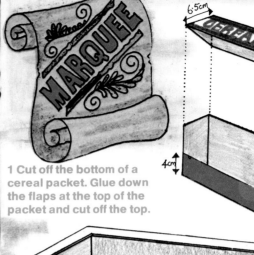

1 Cut off the bottom of a cereal packet. Glue down the flaps at the top of the packet and cut off the top.

These make the base and roof of the marquee. Use the rest of the packet to make flags, helmets etc.
2 Take bottom part of packet and cut out a piece of thin card to cover the back and both sides with an extra 1 cm at each end to overlap the front of the marquee. Mark stripes all along the card using felt tip pen, then glue onto the packet.
Cut out a piece of card to cover the front of the marquee with 1 cm extra along the top to make the edging. Mark stripes along the card.
Turn the card over and colour in the extra 1 cm at the top.
Cut slits along this coloured edge every 1 cm, about 1 cm deep, and round off end flap to make edging. Bend this edge over onto striped side of card and glue onto front of marquee.

FLAGS FENCE AND FEATHERS

1 For flags, glue pieces of coloured card onto cocktail sticks.
2 Jousting fence is two strips of corrugated cardboard 47 cm × 5 cm.

3 Helmets are made from thin card covered in silver paper with an eye slit cut out. Plumes for helmets are strips of crêpe paper, fringed on one side, rolled up and glued.

3 To make the roof, take top part of the packet. Cut out a piece of card to cover both sides of roof overlapping front and back 1 cm Mark stripes along roof and colour the extra 1 cm edging completely. Cut out the edging as before and glue onto roof.
For the ends of the roof, cut out a semicircle of card, colour with stripes and make edging. Cut in half (making two quarter circles) and glue onto ends of roof.

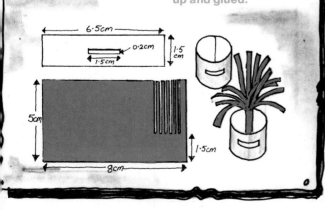

SKI MARATHON

When you try anything for the first time you can expect to feel a bit of a fool. It's something you get used to on Blue Peter. But I wished the snow could have swallowed me up the moment I realised I was *last* in a race of 12,000 skiers! I was trying my luck in the Engadine Ski Marathon—raced over 42 kilometres of Swiss snow.

I was woken up on the day of the race at around 4.30 a.m. by the sound of heavy traffic. Bleary eyed, I peered out of my hotel bedroom window and saw bus after bus after bus going past. Already in the minute I'd been looking out, twenty-five empty buses had gone down the hill towards St Moritz railway station. By half past six, the whole place was packed with buses. The first train arrived and thousands of would-be marathon champions poured out and onto the buses. 12,000 skiers had to get to the start—11,999 people who knew what they were doing—and me!

The race is run from Maloja to Zuoz. When I entered, I didn't even think I'd make the whole run. I've done a bit of downhill skiing, but I discovered that cross-country skiing—langlaufing, to be technical—was quite a different matter.

The ski equipment was the first surprise. The skis were very narrow and instead of big, bulky, tightly clamped ski boots, I was given a pair of what looked like training shoes, except for a lip on the toe—that's where your foot is attached to the ski. And when I was clamped in, I discovered the second big difference between downhill and cross-country skiing—my heel wasn't fixed to the ski. This was so that I could walk and glide on the skis. There was a race to be won and I had to learn a whole new technique of skiing in a hurry.

6.30 a.m.—St Moritz station is packed with buses ready to transport 12,000 skiers to the start of the race.

Zak Freeth and Spud Leaning showed me how to wax my skis for the best grip and fastest slide!

The massed start was signalled by a cannon fired on the side of the valley.

Some skiers had broken down the fence at the start to take a short cut—I followed in their tracks.

The day before the race, I met up with some of the British langlaufers who'd entered for the race, Zak Freeth and Spud Leaning, both majors in the Royal Artillery. Zak used to be a champion downhill skier, but has now turned his skis to cross-country. Spud has been a fan of this sport for many years.

They told me the difference between winning and losing is all down to the wax you put on your skis. It sounded unlikely, until Zak and Spud showed me their box of waxes—dozens of them. Some were specially designed to stop the sliding and give you a good grip on the snow.

You can put several layers of wax on the skis. As the race progresses, the temperature rises and the condition of the snow changes so you need a different sort of wax. You have to gamble, and put your layers of wax on hoping that by the time the temperature rises to say zero degrees centigrade, your below-freezing wax has worn away so that you'll continue to glide energetically along the course. Many a skier has lost a race because he chose the wrong wax—the weather changed suddenly and he was caught with his waxes down!

Zak and Spud offered to wax my skis for me—an offer I grabbed at. The night before the race, they arrived with some unbelievably sticky red wax, like a thick glue, and they smeared it over two-thirds of each ski. It was a messy job—Spud had to smooth it out by hand, which got just as sticky as the ski. On the front and back of the ski, Zak put on a stick wax—this was for speed—I wasn't sure just how much I'd be needing that one!

On the race morning, I met our Swiss camera crew and we left St Moritz for the start at 6.30 a.m. The race wasn't due to start until 9.00 a.m., but we'd been told that it's fairly chaotic up at Maloja and I'd got to be checked in and given my race number—11327. I hoped that would be lucky!

The organisers had done a splendid job. I was given my number very quickly plus a red plastic bag, for anything I didn't want to carry in the race—they'd be ferried to the finish where I'd be able to pick them up—another mammoth task for the race officials. The only thing that seemed a bit on the short side was the number of lavatories—there were queues of several hundred skiers to each of them! Early-morning nerves!

The start was on a frozen lake divided into three pens. The first was for the real experts, the next pen for those who'd done well in the last few marathons, and behind all those came the novices. But I felt they should have a special pen just for me marked: "For the one who's crazy enough to try out a marathon when he's never even tried cross-country skiing before".

By 7 o'clock several thousand skiers were already on the frozen lake. There was still two hours to go before the start, but if you want a good starting position, you have to be there early. The sun still had to climb above the mountain peaks so skiers were dressed in plastic macs, woolly bootees and track suits to keep warm. Jolly Swiss music blared from loudspeakers and we all jigged around in time to it, trying to keep warm.

The minutes ticked by—a giant clock at the start showed that 9 o'clock was approaching. Skiers were crowded all around me—it was like being in a football crowd.

Ten seconds to go—5, 4, 3, 2, 1. A cannon fired—the deafening sound ricocheted round the valley and suddenly 12,000 people moved forward!

Now was the chance for Noakes to show what he was made of—skiers were flashing past me on all sides. Half-way up the start, the fence had been broken down and skiers were getting through the gap, trying to gain a few places. I followed and then I looked up. The race had been going exactly two minutes—and already I was last!

But determined not to give up, I put my best ski forward—found a good, clean set of tracks and chased after the 11,999 in front of me.

After half an hour, the skiers were spread out along the race track for over 5 kilometres! It looked like millions of ants crawling along the bottom of the valley.

At the front, the leaders weren't crawling though—the first two took just 50 minutes to the half-way point—when they finished, just three-tenths of a second would separate them!

Huge milk churns, full of hot soup, were brought to the track side on a sledge.

"Bouillon, bouillon. . . ," cried one small 9-year-old, holding out his cups for the skiers to grab as they shot past. No one actually stopped—they drank as they skied.

I never made it to the soup! After I'd crossed the first frozen lake, my legs were killing me. I knew I'd never reach the finish.

I asked who I thought was a policeman (but it turned out he was a fireman!) how far I'd gone—he said 30 kilometres. I felt quite proud until I realised he'd misunderstood me—*that* was the distance left to go. But I had done 12 kilometres—and that was enough—I was the most shattered langlaufer in the Alps.

I wanted to see the finish, so I hitched a lift with the camera crew. We got to Zuoz and the finishing line at around noon. I thought the race would probably all be over—but there were hundreds and hundreds of skiers arriving.

Every skier was timed for the race. On our backs we'd carried a computer tag. I wouldn't be given a time, but those who reached the end put their tags straight into a timing machine. Their time would help them get a better (or worse!) starting position in next year's marathon.

With the thousands of skiers milling around the finish, I never expected to see Zak or Spud again but incredibly, I literally just bumped into Spud.

"How did you do?" I asked.

"I finished in 2½ hours. How did you do?" he enquired, looking fairly surprised to see me! I owned up and said I'd got to Zuoz by car.

"Don't blame you!" smiled Spud. That made me feel quite a lot better. I rubbed my aching legs and thought: "Those other 11,999 can skim over the mountains without me next year. . . ."

After 3 kilometres I needed a rest! I looked forward to reaching the refreshment stalls for some hot soup, but I never made it!

"Bouillon, bouillon!" shouted this young soup-seller. It's ski as you drink for the "langlaufers"!

When a Swiss fireman told me there were still 30 kilometres to go—number 11327 just had to give up!

TRAPEZE

"He flew through the air with the greatest of ease, That daring young man on the flying trapeze."

That was Top of the Pops more than a hundred years ago, and people then were obviously as thrilled by the glamour of the stars in the most noble, most graceful and most daring of all the circus acts as they are today.

It all began in a swimming bath in France in 1859. One day, the bath attendant tied a piece of wood on to the window cord which hung down from the fanlight, and became the very first man on the flying trapeze. Later, he perfected the act and performed it in his circus, wearing a new outfit which he had copied from a bathing costume. The garment was called after him, as it is to this day. His name was Monsieur Leotard.

The Flying Trapeze is more impressive the more you know about it. The first time you see an act enter the ring in a spotlight, discard their silken cloaks and climb hand over hand with effortless ease to the platform 90ft above the sawdust will quicken your pulse. And if you're lucky enough to see a flyer perform a triple somersault in the air, your heart may

stop for a fraction of a second. But only when you realise that the flyer comes out of that third somersault at the speed of an express train and that a fraction of a centimetre of error on the swing of the catcher could mean a blow in the face like a heavyweight punch, do you begin to understand the art and the daring of the man on the flying trapeze.

But how do you start to learn a skill where a mistake could cost you your life? One cold and frosty day last winter, Lesley and I went to the Billy Smart's Circus winter quarters where some of the younger members of the Smart family were starting to make up a trapeze act. The act was called the Flying Cousins, because that's exactly what they were. Davida and Gabriella Smart, aged fourteen and fifteen respectively, and their cousins, fifteen-year-old Michel and Jean-Pierre Poissonet. Jean-Pierre, who was sixteen, was the oldest and strongest, which made him the obvious choice for "the catcher". The catcher is the lonely one who does most of the work ("when they do one trick each, I do three")—gets the biggest share of the knocks ("if they miss my hands, it's ten to one they hit my head")—the smallest share of the applause ("if you catch him that's good, but he's the one that's done the trick")—and the lion's share of the responsibility ("it's always the catcher who misses the flyer—never the other way round"). I felt an instant sympathy for the catcher, probably because I'm sure that's what they'd ask *me* to do!

I began the long climb up to the cradle where Jean-Pierre Poissonet was sitting sideways on the bar waiting for me, swinging gently from side to side as though he was sitting on a garden gate. Jean-Pierre is in the sixth form at Charters School where he's working up to his 'A' levels. His parents were both in the circus, and that is clearly where his heart is. Mine, at that moment, was in my mouth as I edged my way on to the minute perch by the side of the cradle. I managed to claw myself into a position with my back towards Jean-Pierre which is not the best way to conduct an interview!

"Do you think you could show me how to get into the catching position," I panted to the empty air in front of me. I didn't dare look round, but I felt that if I could get myself locked into the cradle I would be all right. Jean-Pierre was marvellous. He slowly talked me through every foot and hand hold.

"That leg over there . . . Hang on a minute . . . You're all right, Pete . . . Now lift the other leg— slowly—that's it?"

The cradle is the parallel bars which you put your legs between so that when you bend over backwards, you are locked into position with your knees round the leading bar and your feet braced against the back one.

"Straighten your legs outwards, Peter . . . That's right. Push yourself right out—and let go with your hands. Let go with your *hands*! You're quite safe—go on! That's it. Now stretch your arms out—and you're in the catching position. O.K.?"

"What do I do now?"

"Well you've got to take your sweater off to catch somebody—because you need bare arms." (Now he tells me!)

"Just push with your knees—and you'll come up again."

"You are joking!"

"No, just push."

It took every bit of strength I could muster, three attempts, and a helping hand from Jean-Pierre to get me upright again.

To be a catcher you need stomach muscles like iron.

"Gabriella, are you ready?" Latzi Lunas, the trainer, called out from the ring below.

"Yes, ready," called Gabriella.

Latzi gave a tug on the safety rope which went round Gabriella's waist. They weren't going to trust one of the Smart family to my amateur hands and I didn't blame them!

I braced the backs of my knees against the cradle and pushed myself out in space again. I could see Gabriella, upside down to me, poised on tiptoe on the flyer's platform.

"Ready?" she called.

"Yes, ready!" I called back.

"Go!" shouted Latzi—and Gabriella took off. She swung towards me until I could almost touch her and then back across the ring to gain height—this one would be it. Back she came—let go the trapeze—I saw her hands, made a grab—and held!

"No! No! NO!" called Latzi. "Don't catch the

I reached the perch and Jean-Pierre talked me down into the catching position.

"That leg over there—hang on a minute—now lift your leg slowly—that's it!"

"Push yourself right out—let go with your hands—and you're in the catching position—great!"

74

It took me ages to claw my way up to the flying platform, where—hanging on for dear life—I asked Davida and Michel what I was supposed to do next!

hands—it's dangerous—she could slip through. You must hold the *wrists*. Try again!"

He lowered her to the floor on the safety rope and she climbed back on to the flying perch.

"Remember—the wrists, Peter . . . Go!"

This time she swung a little higher, which meant she came off the trapeze faster, but I was able to grab her wrists, and she mine, with the most satisfying thwack.

"Perfect catch," called Latzi. And I must admit I felt pretty good.

I (Lesley) was watching all this from the flying platform with Davida and Michel. Davida told me that they had been practising for seven weeks. She showed me her hands which were covered in blisters.

"They get a bit tougher every day," she said with a smile. "I should be really hardened up in a few weeks' time."

Gabriella rejoined us and I asked her if she'd had any injuries.

"Only a cut head," she said cheerfully. "I had to have stitches, because someone let the trapeze go—and it hit me."

If a trapeze on its own can do that, I thought, what on earth is it like with a man on the end of it!

They tightened up the buckles on my harness, and showed me how to rub my hands with magnesium powder to get a better grip. Jean-Pierre eased himself

back whilst Davida hooked back the trapeze and put the bar firmly in my hands.

"Don't be nervous—nothing can go wrong—just swing out—and let go!"

"Then what happens?"

"Nothing. Latzi will lower you gently to the floor."

Come on, Lesley, I thought. It can't be worse than Bishop Rock! "But you said you'd never do that again," said a still, small voice inside me!

My heart began to thump against my ribs—my mouth was bone dry, and my knees were definitely wobbling.

"Go!" shouted Latzi—and I was off before I had time to reply.

I saw the ring coming up to meet me, and I really don't remember anything else. I was still in one piece so Latzi must have pulled the safety rope at the right moment. I waved to Gabriella, Davida, Michel and Jean-Pierre and went off to find Peter.

As an ex-dancer, I know all about aching muscles, bruises and blisters; and working in television, I know the fears of appearing twice a week in a 'live' programme. But, I thought, as I looked up and saw my trapeze still swinging in the roof of the Big Top, there are worse places to make a mistake than standing on the floor of a television studio.

(speech bubbles:) NO CHEATING · WHO WAS THAT? · I'M SURE I ANSWERED ALL CORRECTLY

PUZZLE PICTURES

1 Larger than life **International Rugby players—Merve the Swerve, J. P. R. Williams** and **Gareth Edwards**—built by John Hughes of Pontypridd.

2 This **35-year-old searchlight** was rescued from a Margate car park. After restoration it will be on display at the Royal Air Force Museum's new Battle of Britain section.

3 The 3, 4 & 5-year-old violin players from the **London Suzuki Group.**

4 The Windsor **"Big Heads",** marching into the Blue Peter studio. This cavalcade of kings raised funds for the Duke of Edinburgh's Silver Jubilee Fund.

5 A **bicycle-powered fireman's helmet** pedalled by the men of Watford Fire Station. The helmet raised a few eyebrows on its charity ride through Holland, Belgium and Germany.

6 The **"Ceremony of the Loving Cup"**—as performed by the Association of Toast Masters.

7 Mac, the 14-month-old collie, was **the first dog ever to play at Headingley.** We telephoned his owner, David Lowery, direct from the Blue Peter studio.

8 Face to face with **Dr Who's K9.**

9 Dancing the charleston in a genuine 1920s' dress.

10 The youngest prize-winner in our **Famous Faces Competition,** 3½-year-old Katherine Daniels, and her portrait of the **Chancellor of the Exchequer, Mr Dennis Healey.**

11 Percy Thrower inspecting **Britain's first tin-can greenhouse,** the invention of Shiu Kay Kan.

(speech bubbles:) HOPE YOU GOT THEM · IS THIS A VITAL CLUE OR JUST A DIRTY MARK · ASK A POLICEMAN

The Case of the Cup that Cheers

1 Bob said that Humphrey had suffered a head injury in Italy, but McMilne claimed to have bandaged his foot.

2 Bob said that Bidchester's players had breakfasted in their hotel at Rosgill, but McMilne said the team was travelling down from Bidchester that morning.

3 The cup final is played at Wembley, and not at White City as McMilne stated.

4 Dickie Davies is an ITV commentator, and does not appear in BBC's *Match of the Day.*

5 It would be impossible for a footballer to play with a broken leg, as any physiotherapist should know.

6 The team travelling from Leicestershire to the south coast would not have driven through East Anglia.

USEFUL INFORMATION

National Deaf Children's Society:
31 Gloucester Place, London W.1.

Brazilian Tourist Board:
35 Dover Street, London W.1.

Kipling's House:
Bateman's, Burwash, Sussex.
Open from end of March to end of September,
14.00-18.00: Closed Fridays.

Madame Tussaud's,
Marylebone Road, London N.W.1.
(Nearest underground: Baker Street)
Open daily 10.00-18.60: Adults £1.20, children 65p.

Knight School:
Chilham Castle, Chilham, Nr. Canterbury, Kent.

BLUE PETER BOOKS

Petra—A Dog for Everyone
By Biddy Baxter and Edward Barnes, published by Pelham Books, £2.95.

The Blue Peter Make, Cook & Look Book
By Biddy Baxter, Hazel Gill and Margaret Parnell, published by BBC Publications, £1.50.

The Blue Peter Book of Limericks
Edited by Biddy Baxter and Rosemary Gill, published by Piccolo/BBC, 40p.

Blue Peter Special Assignments
Rome, Paris and Vienna/Venice and Brussels/Madrid, Dublin and York/London, Amsterdam and Edinburgh/by Edward Barnes and Dorothy Smith, published by Severn House, £2.75.

Paddington's Blue Peter Story Book
by Michael Bond, published by Fontana Lion, price 60p.

Blue Peter Books Nos. 1-14 are now out of print—so hang on to your copies, they may become collectors' items!

ACKNOWLEDGEMENTS

The Man who invented Akela was written by Dorothy Smith; *Souper Spud* and *Lord Nelson's Funeral* were illustrated by Robert Broomfield; and the *Mystery Picture* was by "Tim".

Photographs in this book were taken by Joan Williams, Barry Boxall, John Jefford, John Adcock, Michael Cook, Christopher Rowlands and Paul Wheeler, with the exception of John at the top of Nelson's Column (p.6) by permission of *The Sun*; Portrait of Nelson (p.9) and Kipling (p.43) by the National Portrait Gallery; and Clare Francis and *Accutrac* (p.39) by Clift Jones Associates.

Biddy Baxter, Edward Barnes and John Adcock would like to acknowledge the help of Gillian Farnsworth and Margaret Parnell

(speech bubbles:) THANKS · USEFUL TO KNOW · DESIGN BY JOHN STRANGE

BLUE PETER COMPETITION

Would you like to come to the Television Centre and see the Blue Peter studio? Would you like to meet the Blue Peter team and all the pets?

This could be *your* chance to come to London and meet them all at a special party!

DISAPPEARING CATS

Whatever we're doing in the studio, you can guarantee that either Jack or Jill will disappear! When this photograph was taken, *both* cats were there—but exactly where was Jill? Mark a cross on the picture to show where you think she was.

★ ★ ★ ★ ★ ★

The twenty-four people who put their cross nearest to the correct place will be invited to our

BLUE PETER PARTY

and there'll be lots of competition badges for the runners-up, too!   The closing date: 15 January 1979.

Cut out your entry and send it to:
**Blue Peter Competition,
BBC Television Centre,
London W12 7RJ**
First prize winners and runners-up will be notified by letter.

Name. ....

Address. ....

....

....Age......

77